THE PC

LOUIS DUDEK

DEFINITIVE EDITION

The Golden Dog
Ottawa – Canada – 1998

ISBN 0-919614-82-5 (paperback)

Canadian Cataloguing in Publication Data

Dudek, Louis, 1918-
    The poetry of Louis Dudek: definitive edition

ISBN 0-919614-82-5

    I. Title.

PS8507.U43A6 1998   C811'.54   C98-901331-6
P39199.3.D83A6 1998

Cover Design: The Gordon Creative Group of Ottawa

Typesetting and layout: Arrimage of Montreal

Distributed by : PROLOGUE INC.
                  1650, Lionel-Bertrand Boulevard
                  Tel (450) 434-0306 / 1-800-363-2864
                  Fax (450) 434-2627 / 1-800-361-8088

The Golden Dog Press wishes to express its appreciation to the Canada Council and the Ontario Arts Council for current and past support of its publishing programme.

Printed & bound in Canada

IN PREFACE

This book may be said to be unnecessary, since all the poems in it are already contained in my published books; or it may be considered essential because some of the poems are crumbling in old books, once published in small editions, that are now hard to find—two of them I myself do not possess, and have had to dig up, brown and frail, buried in the local library—and no reader could possibly find all the poems, or recognize them in the surrounding melee and confusion without such a selection.

And then, the poems have been chosen with the thought that a writer should, at some late date in his life, make a selection of his own best work, as a final definition of the art he has struggled with. I have gone through all my books carefully and from them I have taken only those few poems that seem to me satisfying, purely as poems. These are the 'absolute poems', as I see it, and as I have always seen it. Some time later I came upon a statement in Kandinsky's *On the Spiritual in Art* that defines the very same idea: «An Egyptian carving moves us more deeply today than it did its contemporaries; for they judged it with the restrictive knowledge of period and personality. But we judge it as an expression of an eternal art.» It is with this view in mind that I have selected these Poems, out of the rubble of «period and personality,» to represent simply—the essence of poetry.

L.D.

«I believe in the sacredness of the human spirit and in the truth of art one and indivisible... I believe that art has a divine source and that it lives in the hearts of all men who have been illuminated by its heavenly light. I believe that having once tasted the sublime delights of this great art one is forever and fatally devoted to it. And I believe that everyone, through its intermediary, can attain to beatitude.»[1]

Paul Gauguin

---

1   Gauguin epigraph from *Cahier pour Aline*, which he wrote for his daughter some years after her death. Trans. LD.

TABLE OF CONTENTS

from EN MÉXICO (1958)

from LAUGHING STALKS (1958)

from CONTINUATION I (1982)

from ZEMBLA'S ROCKS (1986)

from

UNIT OF FIVE
(1944)

NIGHT SCENE

I meant to be walking in the night-time
But I lean here, for the street is quiet.
It is very still between the buildings.
No one passes.
Somewhere I hear the notes of a piano,
And into my head drift the words of a poem
Which a while ago I was reading.
I notice how the light from a window
Falls upon the snow in the alley;
The street is quite deserted.
Now a man passes,
Making no more sound than a shadow.
Above me a few stars quietly
Stay between the dark houses.

THE DANCERS

One night they played "The Ziegfeld Girl,"
an old revival
I remembered many years for the dance.
I went, and looked at a waltz routine for two
that reeled off like a spool in my mind
    with figures, black and white,
      lights in criss-cross fans along the floor,
and the tic-tac of heels
and tocs of dancers.

Memory opened
    a line of closed shutters in me;
    and made an arc light
to cast figures from a picture-box again.

I touched corners, and looked
at half-cut moons, the weave of arms,
the sudden limbs
    folded like grasshoppers,
    broken, unfolded,
    then soft and supple again;
and always the rays, dazzling, a criss-cross
of light, and the tic-tac of heels
and toes on a stage.

Two dancers, all my life, in me
go dancing; never still nor long poised,
making the complete routine, the tricky choreography;
always restarting at the cue.

Look into my eyes, and hold me by the waist.
Do you see two dancers?
The black and white shadows?
Do you hear the tic-tac of heels
    and toes of dancers?

AT PARTING

Know, that as a rose unpetals in the morning
So your lips unpetal under my lips;

And also, like a bird sleeping with wings folded,
Your eyelids sleep under my kisses.

But like a road running through cornfields
Is the length of your arm when you are saying good-bye;

And like a city crumbling, in ruin,
Is my emotion when the the door closes.

Like a streetcar, like a terrible tractor,
It is all rumbling and tumbling in me when you are gone.

TROIS VERS

J'ai écrit trois vers comiques
Pour Fernande petite et chic,
Pour Fernande que j'adore
Trois vers sonores.

Et j'ai reçu ma récompense
Car j'ai vu avec jouissance
Fernande rire de mon poême,
Fernande que j'aime

Quand je songe maintenant
À nos délicieux moments
Je vois encore Fernande lire,
J'entends son rire.

THE SEA

I

Ghostlike against the sun
You stand, and scan
A track upon the flood,
Glistering, gone.

Your thin arm raised
To the bright sea
Is knife-like against
Reality

And warm, lost man,
Like solar light
You make globed worlds,
And dread the night;

Or think of sped time
Run like a glass,
Where the bright road
Vanishes,

For each ray mirrors
A split past,
And fiction disappears
In plain glass.

II

From change to still memory
Water widens,
And in its breathless air
No man hides;

Distinct in white sun
With rooks and towers,
Peopled and green, flee
The far shores.

Adrift in the fast flood
Of present light,
There is no shade from final
Sun's sight:

All vision in the eyes
Of love gone.
Is hurt by the quick, material
Glance of sun;

And maidens with spun hair
And lips red
Bleed like a blood weed
Their thin blood.

Think of a pale girl
You once loved,
And held by a small wrist
Imprisoned.

Your once caught vision
Of white linen
Wet with her tears like rain,
Abandon:

Seek for new ilots
Of hurt desire,
        Where shed sunlight prances
A fresh fire.

If there is bitter truth
To taste and swallow,
Know that the same gruel
Is medicine and food.

Death itself is curable
In the human body,
Though one generation find
No near recovery.

III

O Hear the voice of the wind!
The sun is down,
He splays the waves where, your bright
Visions drown!

Hear the night wind
On a spumed sea,
How he gathers the scud and breaks
It menacingly.

In the dark, whirling wave
Is a green home,
Quiet and secret anchor
For tired bone...

O listen to the wind
In a dour sky,
How it masks the sharp glint
Of a star's eye.

Seek, sail! O seek
The lost land:
Shatter your bones along
The lone strand.

Though wink the sunny islands
Eyes have seen,
They will vanish in mirage,
Sharp and keen,

And foot will feel no shores
That man found
Mirrored in glassy ikons
Of the mind;

But like thin, springtime edges
Of ice in sea
Will vanish where long grass
Waves silently,

Where on the floor of oceans
Tiered and reefed

Rise in flower and in coral
Cities in the deep.

There, drifted at last, hands
Moveless fold,
And eyes the liquid limes
Lave and remold

To keep there for ageless
Time entombed,
The chemistry of flesh
Sealed and fused;

Till barebacked, whole, and hard,
Rending the deep,
Leviathan continents shall rise
Where oceans sleep,

And portals your lime and clay
Shall open apart,
In cities high with wonder
Of heroic art...

O for these, the cities,
(Hear the wind!)
Shall the fire of your bones
Be cold, be stilled.

from

EAST OF THE CITY
(*1946*)

ROMANTIC LYRIC

The cloth-white ferns on these winter windows
remind me of Monday mornings, and frozen washing
and billows of bubbling steam
which would be rising from the doorways: I remember
     it all,
as I stand at this window and watch the wind blow.

O, but the weather's changed!   I see the wind more
than the ferns, and I am more cold than I was then.
I do not love the warmth indoors either;
no more, waiting thin before the window
while there, a white thing
something I have imagined and loved
falls like a cold fluttering bird.

EVENING

The noise of these buildings
quietens down.
The rage of these busy streets
dies down and becomes still.
The hardness
softens, and is forgotten
when the lamps fade
and silently the dark gathers
on the walls.

HER VOICE COMES TO ME

Her voice comes to me
not from the cold winter
not from the distance
but from within me,

and when I hear her laughter
I think of the thin, thin leaves
she touches, the blossoms
she breathes on, and how she leans
and laughs when she speaks

for her voice is like a young fiddler
echoing in me, in a tree's shade.

from

THE SEARCHING
IMAGE
(*1944*)

OLD MUSIC

We make our freedom in the laws we make,
And they contain us as the laws we break
Contained a remnant of an ancient music
That a new music in its laws contains.

You played, and struggled with a glorious law.
And there your energy with love I saw
Wresting a rhythm out of rocks of air
Always as Bach himself had put it there;

But what had made him free now kept us bound
In a closed prison, in a room of sound—
Until you played it so time's rust did ring
With the glow of freedom that it once could bring.

And then the rhythm leaped out of your hands,
Leaped in the air in protoplasmic strands.
Breaking old laws, the silence of the tomb.
Breaking the ribs and murals of your room:

Until the shadow of the form he made
Spread in the air and touched things like a shade—
Bach's shade, who carved it and had made the laws
Whose echo from our bondage such freedom was.

CLOUDS

Pale from the storm's mouth
the white clouds move out,
they slowly turn
like hills of clouded ice
or winter glass before our eyes.
Under their shadows burn
battered buildings ashamed,
tenements under East River
under a project of new homes;
the flapping fringes of the city
cower and cover their knees and bones.
But the clouds arc not sad
on this account. Can it be that,
somewhere, they see beyond
mountains and green lands?
They move like the Greek philosophers,
wreathed in smiles,
as if the knowledge of love
and timeless peace made them mild.

FLOWERS ON WINDOWS

Flowers bloom in the window pots in sprays
of softness, or pointed like pain—waves of violets,
stiff chrysanthemums, bugles, bells of red:
against the walls they are the life that answers,
they are the dwellers, and the rest is dead.

Men move mountains and build their cities;
and yet, the only answer I would like to find,
the fact the mind would embrace as a lover
and would greedily uncover under the design—
is the city built within him that moves a man!

Though lost in the ignorant traffic, I would yet rejoice.
There is some hidden wisdom in all gardens,
cities, in the leaves of flowers, the eyes of boys!
The dog is not reckless of that message, nor
are the men and women rattling through the stores.

All moves with a hidden meaning; only the fool
denies God (even as the priest-fool simplifies).
Tell me, should we see in the revolving seasons
mathematics? in the weather, circulating air?
Or the answer, then, in any book, or prayer?

What is there in man which builds a city?
And where the original city he began?
I have ravaged the womb, and the planted seed,
and moved mountains of knowledge for this gold.
Now look upon the surface—how these flowers unfold!

THE POMEGRANATE

The jewelled mine of the pomegranate, whose hexagons of
    honey
The mouth would soon devour but the eyes eat like a
    poem.
Lay hidden long in its hide, a diamond of dark cells
Nourished by tiny streams which crystallized into gems.

The seeds, nescient of the world outside, or of passionate
    teeth,
Prepared their passage into light and air, while tender roots
And branches dreaming in the cell-walled hearts of plants
Made silent motions such as recreate both men and fruits.

There, in a place of no light, shone that reddest blood,
And without a word of order, marshalled those grenadiers:
Gleaming without a sun—what art where no eyes were!—
Till broken by my hand, this palace of unbroken tears.

To wedding bells and horns howling down an alley.
Muffled, the married pair in closed caravan ride;
And then, the woman grown in secret, shining white,
Unclothed, mouth to mouth he holds his naked bride.

And there are days, golden days, when the world starts to
    life,
When streets in the sun, boys, and battlefields of cars,
The colours on a bannister, the vendors' slanting stands
Send the pulse pounding on like the bursting of meteors—

As now, the fruit glistens with a mighty grin,
Conquers the room, and, though in ruin, to its death
Laughs at the light that wounds it, wonderfully red.
So that its awful beauty stops the greedy breath.

And can this fact be made, so big, of the body, then?
And is beauty bounded all in its impatient mesh?
The movement of the stars is that, and all their light
Secretly bathed the world, that now flows out of flesh.

COME ON, MR. FREUD

I dreamed that was sitting with God on my knees
While three unhappy banged men whistled in the trees;
A stream was flowing by of curdled blood and milk
With a lady in the current wrapped in blood-stained silk.

"O God you giant turtle," I sang Him a lullaby,
And then, sourly distorted, I heard God cry;
He changed as I heard Him into a lump of fat,
Then vanished—I was sitting in my pale straw hat.

The dark sky lifted and began to shine,
The trees sprouted leaves and a flowering vine,
The hanged men, now bananas, ripened in the sun,
And a dead-fish carcass seemed a red-cross bun.

The girl drowned in purple awoke from her dream,
The milk turned to water, the blood to pebbles green;
We kissed by the river, I held her finger-tips;
A bird came down and took seed from her lips.

The wind played in the branches, happy as if insane,
And the birds chirped gaily in the brittle cane;
I kissed and held her, and laughed without a sound,
While God, the great turtle, rumbled underground.

FLOWER BULBS

Most men give flowers in their full leaves,
But I give you flowers still in seed:
These flowers you see are each one wrapped
In the womb, still concentrated in sap.

Think, what I lay on your fearless palm!
A universe compacted to a seeming chaos,
A wary cell waiting to split its tomb
In birth, when the soon-rampant seed explodes.

Yet we generate such, and once were seeds:
Have blossomed once like flowers inside a girl;
Now sit with hanging hands and open eyes,
Nourished by, not knowing, the objective world.

And this which is closed to younger eyes
Only loving you could have opened to me.
I have walked by many a garden in a room
And passed by many a precipice being blind.

Yet love may tell one who grows a plant
How a miraculous ignorance surrounds
Each living thing—and it still be
Perfect and wise, and beautiful as a bud.
So you and I, when these plant leaves appear
Like days unfolding in the calendar,
Will watch the flowers sent out in shoots
And love grow out of his mysterious roots.

THEME AND VARIATIONS

Leaving the waters of the splendid East, the sun leaps up into the firmament to bring light to the immortals and to men who plough the earth and perish.

The sun moved over the fields like a brand of fire over men and women harvesting in Massachusetts while the city gods lay on their backs sleeping.

Like a room-ripened fruit, tasteless, unbeautiful, the pink orb appeared in the alley; cats crawled away into corners; boots grated on the concrete. In the fierce furnaces a kind of thunder rattled: the gods were almost remembered.

Through venetian blinds, on the silk settee, the sun landed like a kitten. An eyelid stirred on the pillow, stayed shut. A murmur as of coffee simmering purred in the corridor from the kitchen.

Awakened in pain to the dull daylight, a woman saw the sun's first agony at the dusty window; and unable to lie still, she rose up trembling, supported by kindly death walking beside her.

Like a buzz of a million bees, the sun woke a head full of fever and swept the tabletop of stiff whisky bottles. Holding his head, the man poured seltzer into a glass of water.

The early sun slashed the newspapers falling from the assembly; like a frantic dog torn from his leash he licked the pages but could not touch the ink nor one syllable of the words that seal the eyes and make the tongue thick and foolish.

Under the rays of the pale morning sun the people pass to the streetcars and busses. He touches them with his light and dries them like summer flies which appear at sunrise, are ignorant and busy and perish with the sunset.

LINE AND FORM

The great orchestrating principle of gravity
            makes such music of mountains
as shaped by the mathematical hands
      of four winds, clouds
            yield in excellent and experimental sculpture;
mushrooms, elephants
      and women's legs, have too their form
            generated within a three-dimensional space
                  efficiently.

And so the emotions
      combine into exquisite
            counterparts of the mind and body
when the moving principle and the natural limits imposed
            work against each other,
                  give in, and resist.

The form is then the single body
            of love that two wrestlers make.
But has each one his own?
                  or is one?
What essential form has
                  a wind or the sky
that cutting into each other
                  they mimic living arms?

Eternal forms.
The single power, working alone
      rounds out a parabola
            that flies into the infinite;
but the deflected particle
            out of that line, will fetch a frisk
                  of sixes and eights
                        before it vanishes:

an ocean arrested
　　　　by sudden solid
　　　　　　ripples out in the sand.

So this world of forms, having no scope for eternity,
　　　　　　is created
　　　in the limitation of what would be complete and
　　　　perfect,
achieving virtue only
　　　　　by the justness of its compromises.

from

CERBERUS

(1952)

POEM FOR SPRING

Mother Earth's belly is broken,
      the spring begins.
Sap flows into deadened arteries,
      branches open,
the lamb bleats, the pussy willow
      puts out;
green is her blood—
      the white scab of winter is washed away.

O let this new birth be
      into a fertile year!
Let the summer fruit be a full scrotum
      between the desired branches
and not fall to the ground,
      wrinkled apples.

Let the horn of morning
      awaken sleeping feathers
        all the long summer,
and if winter comes,
      let it be a sleep
hungry, and dreamful
      of unforgotten spring.

A CHILD BLOWING BUBBLES

Against the storefronts, by the loud busses whose
blue exhaust in its clean coloured worlds
made moving clouds and many a blossoming rose,
the child laughed, blowing its small breath
into a curved wire, a magic circle for a cent.

Blowing more, and catching the globes, it laughed
at me bemused in wheels of floating foam,
crisp and crystal fortune balls about my head—
when looking at the future there I lost my thread
of childlike sense, and brutish saw each bubble burst.

FOR E.P.

For Christ's sake, you didn't invent sunlight;
There was sun dazzle before you, and stricken leaves,
Phoibos of the goddamned "narrow thighs" —
But you talk as if you made light or discovered it.

SUBURBAN PROSPECT

Blue, blue above the prim
    houses where tea roses nestle and birds'
        swift penmanship
  runs across a lawn and a live maple:
asters, hedgerows, a yellow tree
    brinded against the sky, and the houses
flawless — no cottage hanging with vine
      and with time overgrown, but a Disney
      design for living, a crêpe-garden at a modern door—
which a fidgety sparrow like a child at a funeral
      is too much alive to know.

Here, coming at evening, you will see
      Smoking Camels on the highway, and
    Chesterfields ahead; maybe a Sky Chief
      sign overhead —
you'll think of these as real and not instead —
General Foods will bring you wholesome breakfast
     every day, a Child's
    Cafeteria will serve you sunshine
      from a tray: you will be wiser
    and buy Kayser, you will be smart
      and be thrifty
and live on less than it would cost a saint to die.

So living in a picture postcard
    of hyaline trees and hedges,
the fizz of waterfalls coming to you from whisky and lime,
in a land of Better Homes and Gardens,
    a scent of cement and tiles...
Any day, or any evening
    (when the birds are making most noise),
      you'll walk home to roses
hanging on your trellis, open the lock of love
    with Liberty in your pocket, Life under your arm.

PRATINAS AGAINST
THE FLUTE
(LITERARY SQUABBLES CIRCA 500 B.C.)

What's this blasted racket? What's all the commotion?
What rough-house ribaldry
    around Dionysus' foot-battered altar?
Stand back, stand back! I'm the priest of boisterous
    Bacchus,
        I'll sing for him...
as if I were among the Naiads on the hills,
or a cool swan singing her motley-feathered moon song.
That's the music. I've made a lot of it
for my Pierian queen, the Muse. So let the flute-players
                follow
ass-wise after me, like servants;
    or better, let 'em get off to the taverns
with young boozers that go bellying doorposts
           in early morning hours.
Smash that snake-spotted pipe! To the flames
with their blah-blah-blathering
    hither-thithering doggerel medleys—
spit-sputtering pig-whistles from a stool-maker's bore!

Here is the movement
        of hand and foot
      fitting words to music...
O Lord of thriamb and dithyramb, ivied Bacchus,
listen to my Doric choriambics!

APPARITION

In blue moonlight, helmeted,
         bronze under the wall,
Her marmoreal arms
         enshrined in grenadine,
White silk, blue smoke
         flowing about her
    and the shadows plying at her feet
                   (as though a sea)
With bossed breast-plate of silver
         armour of love,
A woman, with will to command—
A goddess? — clean out of nowhere
In a dark night, by the dark ball-park stadium
Came to me, saying,
         "I desire of thee that love
             thou hast not shown.
         Thou art called."
Called. She turned. Armour
         glint on her shoulders, the hair massed
                   under helmet —
A goddess? And the surge of the dark upon her.
I stood there, sight chasing down alleys,
         fearful, uncouth
    in my ignorance, tongueless
         as though to speak were forbidden.
And now I am ashamed.
Was it some love she called me to?

LOVERS

The daughters of the moon and sun
Have shoulders like green apples
And mouths of flame:
The sons of thunder lie with them

In the magnetic mountains.
Rivers of mercury trickle down the rocks
Where the maidens lie on the mosses
With the boys born out of lightning.

ALBA

As you lay on the bed pale with
                    the humid breath of kisses
          still moist on your cheek, openly,
like a leaf your water-lily limbs,
                    the river, past the bed, to the sea
          below, to the city, dragged down our two
selves, slowly, down, to the sound of
                    cataracts in the street below, in
          humming early morning light.

DANGER

The poet, living in a cloud of violent dream,
congested with energy,
illuminates only as lightning does, fitfully,
with less light than thunder;
he flings plums at your feet as if they were boulders.
You will not learn from him of your danger,
you must fear a more mean and mechanical murder—
Greed, with arithmetic in his fangs, coils near you,
his tail in time and the grave;
you can hardly hear his sliding as he crawls
among the shining faces of the dead and living who sleep.

from

TWENTY-FOUR
POEMS
(*1952*)

FAIR CALYPSO

Love came like a midnight fever
        And went away—
                night wind with the dawn.

Now the days are quiet
        islands in a dark sea.

Tell me,
        where is that storm?
        Where is the wave that carried me
            to her side?

AN AIR BY SAMMARTINI

It was something you did not know
        had existed— by a dead Italian.
Neither words nor a shape of flesh
        but of air;
            whose love it celebrated
           and "cold passion"
Amoroso Canto, a crystal
        that fell from musical fingers—
As a cloud comes into the eye's arena,
        a certain new tree
           where the road turns,
        or love, or a child, is born,
           or death comes:
Whatever s found or is done
        that cannot be lost or changed.

PURE SCIENCE

Poetry is a man-made kite
                skating on an imaginary sky,
But nobody knows what the sky is
                nor why there are kite-makers.

It is also like grandmother's idea of heaven
                that we have learned to do without
Because nobody cooks there,
                sleeps with girls, or mints money.

It is a whirling
                spark in a vacuum,
And only scientists seem to
                enjoy the experiment.

AT THE ROUND WINDOW

Between the apartment's glass glittering windows,
in the jungle of a tree,
arrested time with a fluttering of the branches
rests unchangeable in our protean age—
like silence cupped in a human hand.
And at the tree's feet
the sparrows brush the pathway
with wings a blaze of action:
old as a wave on a stone, they break with panic life.
And they have hopped, since the first and earliest bird,
and cell-like move in an infinite wide pattern
in the microscopic wafer of a slide,
while we build a changing sky of glass.
Does there beat in the breast of every bird
the same novelty and discovery,
as if he, the first bird, and only true bird,
breathed this life, found this leaf?

from

EUROPE
(1954)

POEM 2

This is not yet the sea, it is the river.
For a long time we have been
only on the river, the rocking-horse waves
of a minor reality, Newton's invention:
roof slates on a mechanical surface,
dollar bills of green, small froth of holiday beer
                    and ice-cream soda.

The river between green banks
holds in the mocked tide
beyond Quebec, beyond Megantic, Restigouche.
Dotted with Donald Duck villages
the shore mounts like a flapjack
on either side. Bridged here and there by cantilevers,
scooped by the dredger, man.

Nowhere is it so noisy, nowhere so unnatural & noisome
as (singing some yoo-ooo love song)
here on this river; yet it is the realest thing,
your present, a gift of time,
the tamed moment of eternity
                    for you,
flowing on and out into the sea, where we go.

4

The biggest waves in this water
are those we make ourselves.

But why fish
in someone else backwash?

There was a time when I was satisfied
with fishing in the clean Sr. Lawrence,
the Little Jesus River
          (no sooner Souster heard it
                    but he put it in a poem),
whiskered bullheads, sweet slim perches,
soup fish in summer.
'Ça mord-t-il?' we used to shout
          to the fishermen under the bridge.

A plodding sport, for the trivial imagination,
                    of waiting, waiting —
then it comes, a small civilized
                              fish
that dies practically in your hand.

Can you live — or die — for such pleasure?
If you have grown to manhood
          and strong reaching desire?

10

But I had not known the sea would be this splendid
         magnificent lady:
'destroyer of ships, of cities'
in luxurious ermine and leopard coat
            sighing in the ship's wake;

destroyer of civilizations, or pantheons,
to whom Greece and Rome are only a row of white
    breakers
spilled with a hush, in air,
then marbled patterns on a smoother wave...

And I would not be surprised if the sea made Time
in which to build and to destroy
as it builds these waves and indolently breaks them,
         or if the whole fiction
of living were only a coil in her curvature
           of immense imagination.

Maker and breaker of nations, sea of resources,
you have enough here for a million rivers,
           for a billion cities,
enough for new Judaea, for flew Alexandria,
and Paris once again, and America's morning.

14

Collumbus with all kinds of cockeyed notions
just had to keep on going and he was sure to find it,
the alchemists with all kinds of cockeyed notions...
Explore the sea for any reason,
            and you are bound to come upon treasure.
Keep active, persist in folly,
just keep on going,
            keep mixing, even with your hands.
The sea has everything, it's the globed universal belly
                bulging with wombs.

19

The commotion of these waves, however strong, cannot
            disturb the compass-line of the horizon
nor the plumb-line of gravity, because this cross
                    coordinates the tragic pulls of necessity
that chart the ideal endings, for waves, and storms
                and sunset winds:
the dead scattered on the stage in the fifth act
— Cordelia in Lear's arms, Ophelia, Juliet, all silent —
show nature restored to order and just measure.
                    The horizon is perfect,
and nothing can be stricter
than gravity; in relation to these
                the stage is rocked and tossed,
kings fall with their crowns, poets sink with their laurels.

A city is a kind of ship,
most of it an old tramp
most of it salt-eaten
sea-stained, encrusted
with lives beyond recall;
some of it new
decked with modern apartments
flying flags and bunting
for life's excursion pleasures;
much of it freight and trade.

A city is a kind of ship,
it touches the ports of time —
Past and Present —
the wharves of space
— Here and Now — it comes and goes
making its long voyage
and then sinks in the sand:
Troy, Ecbatan, buried cities.

34
COVENT GARDEN

What the head of the schoolboy heard
who held his ear against the prima donna's breast
all the time that she sang her aria:
the source of all music,
    a noise in the shelled heart of a woman.
She flung her notes against the prows of druid rocks
and they echoed back to us.
        For time is a great wall
to carry echoes, whatever we see or hear.
This is London. Tonight
there are two musics — in Covent Garden
and in Whitehall, the auditorium of power.
But to hear the first sound, where they are one,
that would be more than music.

40

There is something in being again on water,
            I ask the white sea
if there is life anywhere
as foaming, as glowing green, as this;
            if land can possibly be, or have,
ever, all that the sea contains.
Monuments fool us, delude us into believing
            that once there was energy
married with equity, to raise such buildings.
But there also was pride and oppressive power,
there also (a dungeon, stocks and irons) they built for
    killing.
The commonplace and the brutish, serf and master
and proud priest; rotting straw on thatched roofs,
slit homestead walls of an ancient farm—
this dirt of the past may as well be cleaned out.
Why should we ride into eight hundred years ago
            to see others as foul as ourselves?
If now only the proud cathedrals remain,
                        it is because art
outlives inhumanity.

History is really the study of failures,
                        the best buildings
lack some points of proportion, dimension.
Only the sea makes her circle perfect.

41

Across the level fields of France
extensive as empire or continent
                    the wind over the wheat
runs in delicate timid waves, moonlit in daytime.

They cultivate every acre
            with geometrical exactitude
as they built their cathedrals with grace.
            We found this true.

The beautiful mind of the cultivated Frenchman
                must be like these fields, these waves,
an undulation measured like the dance
                    of Cleopatra's body.

49

Only in Chartres, under the dome
      (two towers, and three windows
      such as God had not seen before)
and the Virgin everywhere, and in the centre
      looking into the nave
streaming with colour so that you almost weep,
      so that you sit
for half an hour in one place, under the dome,
      looking four ways,
under the dome of Chartres
      (about which I cannot speak,
      have really no right to talk)
I knew in the very centre what had gone wrong
    in Paris, and understood Versailles.
'How could they give up this?'
'Entertainment, amusement, have eaten up the arts!'
And fossil French classicism, which France cannot outlive.
Exhibitions of the rich, debasing ancient art
      for female self-adornment and display—
like the phylloxera, have eaten at the root.
For which they have abandoned Chartres.

50

The Greeks were fine, but French classicism
using the Greek for its own purpose,
smooth hypocrisy, conceit, & the display
                    of that corruption, *le bon goût,*
—the worst taste in manners or in art
                    the world has ever seen—
spoiled two centuries of European art,
opened the arts to worse corruption still—
                    the monstrous sugar teeth
of 'money' and 'amusement': here you see
                                    in Chartres
art is no entertainment, it does not amuse;
money paid for it, but it paid for
                    something that the sculptor really preferred;
pride was satisfied, but it was pride
                    in objects, the full scale
of human performance—they worked for this, gladly.
The wedge of ignorance entered Europe
                    with a blind idolatry
of Greece and Rome; you can see it
            as a straight line from the fifteenth century down,
'art for art', copying the Greek forms,
shape without sense, imitating
                    imitations, dramatic motion, sensuality
for the boudoir, decorativeness
to make room for gold, for size.
After this, there was no honesty
whether in art or trade, to fight off the incisor
of the pure profiteer, the hog
with his snout in the mire, his belly in shit.
The Gothic tower had fallen,
                            the last craftsman
dropped his hammer; it has come
to all of us, poets, advertisers,
dance hall singers and all,

we make our pilgrimage to Chartres, without praying
        beads;
look at the Virgin helpless, and up to the great dome
        where the light seems to rise and fall.

53

Under the rocks at Biarritz
where the sea rushes in, in terraces
        of white breakers
toward the tourists scattered on the crisp spattered sand—
the two protagonists of this epos,
        the latter creating
hotel fronts
& zebra umbrellas
as usual;
the sea carving the architraves of the ragged rocks.

Beauty is a form of energy.

When that is depleted, pleasure
        or comfort, is all that the organism desires.
The apparent energy of the factories
        and industrial sites, so ugly,
        which we have seen in France and in England
        (the length and breadth of them)
is really exhaustion, not power, so far as the worker
        is concerned, in his dismal dwellings;
despair because there is no beauty.
And the masters of that system, whom we can now see, if
        [we want to,
        will be brutal beings, desperate
in their ignorant search for enjoyment and power;
they cannot be dedicated
or happy in the expression
        of their virility,
nor feel in their veins the sea as they work.

59

Where the sea smashes
        on the rocks at Bordighera:
simply for pleasure,
           like the surf at Sete,
                alone, for miles and miles
           of wind and sea-washed
                      sand

a strip of land, where there is water on both sides
and a good road running by the sea—
lonely, we stopped and stripped
for the sweet salt surf, the sea
        that took us in as though we were nothing
           (making that poem)

or on the glittering Riviera
        (hard pebbles, but good water)
where there are 30 miles also devoted entirely to pleasure,
we rested at any rate, one afternoon
           and slept there
(the Casino stupid and vulgar,
one could see the money
        raked in by the croupier,
and very little coming back)
or at *baccarat*, each betting against the other
        the House always collecting its dividends.
No art out of this, says Ezra,
there is no art where there is theft on the community
and each bets against the other.
No art in St. Raphaël,
        Nice or Cannes,
a hundred years later, 200 years later
these villas will lie in ruin
still an eyesore
        & the money and the bankers
                no more
(says, or might say, Ezra);

but we enjoyed it
lying on the beach there and sleeping
after Spain, the fiesta,
after the ruins of Villafranca,
             the caves of Les Baux,
                vineyards, the grape country
of Spain and France, equally good,
          and the small towns of Provença.

Lay by the sea sleeping
with the Casino overhead,
       and the sea lapping quietly at our feet.

62

In the middle of the night they burst out singing,
like drunken men everywhere, I thought,
        and your nerves were overwrought;
but they had a guitar, & the player was no slouch,
and they loved their songs, though the wine
            had unstrung their voices;
it was this also that I had expected
     (kept us awake for an hour),
like the people of Pamplona dancing,
the art that is better than poetry
          or even the oldest ruins—
the art we dream of in the others.

66
ROME

The present is all too present
and the past all too past:
streetcars and Roman crowds, a monstrous static
      of old echoes and new noise.
I cannot hear my own heartbeat,
how should I hear what falls
from the columns of the Twelve Gods
or the hoarse whispers that grow like moss
on the stumps of the Rostra?
Rome was not built in a day; but a day is enough
once it is over, to make an end to Rome.
Nothing has power that was only power
when it lived and had its will; only the power
that is married to beauty survives. Virgil was not satisfied
with his epic when he died, nor Marc Aurelius
      that he was wise.
We may learn from this how the hours should be adorned
      with leaves
and the columns of days garlanded.

70

We have seen bits of this marble
        scattered over all the cities of Europe:
how could it be entire? What Greece has given,
and been robbed of, was so much
        they have left nothing for themselves—
           a beggared people, cheating the tourists
on every menu, smiling insidiously,
        living now without cleanness, without order,
surrounded by deserts, the pinkish-white mountains
           parched by the sun,
that one must cross, to Delphi, to Mycenae,
to the cape over the sea at Sunion.

Time and the wars have destroyed it all, but the Acropolis
standing there, crumbling with infinite slowness,
           in the sunlight,
is all that it ever was, will be, until the last speck
of the last stone is swept away by the gentle wind.
Strange, that a few fragile, chalky, incomplete blocks of
               [marble,
        worn away by time, thievery, and gunpowder,
should be enough, and all that we have come for,
to erect in the mind the buildings
of the Greeks who lived here, and their city—
akro-polis against the blue sky of heaven.
I have said of the sculptures, such people
will never again be, it is more
        than we can really believe in.
Shall we ever again see such buildings? Heaven
        seemed near then so that the hand could touch it.
But we have the light years,
           the immeasurable solitudes.
I sit here, drinking in sunlight
from the clean candid marble,
        thinking the thoughts of Plato,
of Solon, and the perfect republic.

74

But we have seen the country people,
an old man and a younger,
the boy with his arm around the elder's neck,
and a spectre-thin woman with a bundle,
     fragile bones under delicate skin,
          dark-eyed, long-suffering,
and men of fine character, with long moustaches,
               quiet, thoughtful,
and women working in the fields,
   the arms moving beautifully at their labour—
among the olive trees, among the grape vines,
rocky soil, dry, the farms poor and infertile,
but the people patient, inured to suffering, weather-beaten,
indifferent to the capitalist or the communist future,
to the rise or fall of cities,
         arts and civilizations,
indifferent to all but the harvest, war with the soil
        and the weather:
these the peasants, who come before and after.

83

As for democracy, it is not just the triumph
          of superior numbers,
but that everyone, continually,
should think and speak the truth.
What freedom is there in being counted among the cattle?
The first right I want is to he a man.
It takes a little courage.
The plain truth, I say, not a few comfortable formulas
that conceal your own special lies;
the simple facts everybody knows
are so, as soon as you bring them to the light.
Democracy is this freedom, this light
shining on the human mind,
                   light
in faces, actions—
as the Greeks once carved it in these stones.

89

In mountains, which are the white-flecked breakers
of the land, so huge the eyes become ocean-hollows,
we see what dimensions these things aspire to.
Beyond imitation. Yet whatever is essential
                                    to humanity,
is to be seen in a few mountainous endeavours—
                    a Leonardo, an Aristotle.
As in Switzerland, it is efficiency
                    which the mountains have given
for emulation: freedom, and relief from the savagery
                    of wars.
In these Alps you will find
tiny blueberries — that we picked by St. Gotthard—
                    and Swiss watches,
both very excellent.
                The size of things
is not to be measured, but by the imagination.

93

We ran into a heavy sea, leaving England,
fog, and unshapely waves, scythed cruelly by the wind;
the torrent passing under us then,
                          black, fearful,
was like a curtain suddenly; the awful ocean
                  closed on the continent,
blotted out Europe, the fortified walls of Cherbourg,
lights of refineries, helpless houses:
a luminous green ran under us, streaming, swirling
— I saw as in a mirror, through a manhole,
a small fishing smack tossed to and fro on the water.
Can they go on living?
                  The sea has washed out
everything I have written, the fiction of temporaneity:
we are back with the real, the uncreated
chaos of ocean,
which will not stop to spare us
                  a regret for all we have lost and forgotten.

94

Today it is cool and refreshing.
.........The sea is almost still,
ice-bright, hard and sun-glazed. Europe is gone.
.........One begins to have some perspective.
.........Like the dead, we remember
the symbolic events that mattered:
.........the red roofs of Chartres
as seen from the cathedral
.....where the schoolchildren sang in unison
sitting at lunch on the green; a boy we befriended in Spain
who wanted to learn from a grammar
.........how to speak the English tongue;
a priest on a bicycle; the Italian girls on the train
who said with their eyes that 'love
is better than money'; the young man in the church
at Lancaster, and the woman who prayed
in Mainz: all these are remembered
in the first effort to return, to relive in memory
what was too little comprehended. Life, like poetry,
can only be understood through comparison, what results
is the perfect, unchanging essence,
.........an eidolon of the good.

95

The sea retains such images
        in her ever-unchanging waves;
for all her infinite variety, and the forms,
inexhaustible, of her loves,
she is constant always in beauty,
        which to us need be nothing more
    than a harmony with the wave on which we move.
All ugliness is a distortion
of the lovely lines and curves
        which sincerity makes out of hands
            and bodies moving in air.
Beauty is ordered in nature
        as the wind and sea
shape each other for pleasure; as the just
know, who learn of happiness
        from the report of their own actions.

99

And so we have arrived.
It narrows into the thin St. Lawrence.
Yet a river with a city inside it,
                with a thousand islands,
as Cartier found it,
as Cabot discovered (I saw his face
                in the Ducal Palace in Venice).
We have had our physical heroes,
and are also a nation
built in the middle of water.
Somehow a bigger place than we left it:
a country with certain resources,
                and a mind of its own, if lacking hunger.
The mountains of Gaspé doze, reclining,
                in the air vacant as morning.
At home, there will be faces full of this daylight,
                blank maybe, but beautiful.
Getting started is never easy.
We have work to do.
                Europe is behind us.
                America before us.

from

THE TRANSPARENT
SEA
(*1956*)

THE PINEAL GLAND

The pineal gland, that was once an eye
on the skull's prow,
dreams now over bales of brain
behind the brow—
dreams of the sea it once knew
when it was young,
and in the darkness still as brave
rocks over thought as on wave.

IN THIS SHINING WATCH

In this shining watch, our mechanistic universe,
whose jewels are the trembling stars,
whose casing is earth, and springs the beating brain,
we must know what time we tell in the light of day
hung in what pendulous spaces—
or the eye's glass will glisten and lose perspective,
whether looking for a needle lost in hay
or for larger regions of clockwise justice.

Knowing this, knowledge may come easier
and touch off the fighting flame;
but without it, even salvation, a new society,
is a pale land, good for ghosts,
and no one cares, or wants the ticking kingdom.

THE CHILD

The tripping of a girl just eight years old,
      a skyward leaping
up from the arches and the tiny thighs
in swings, like flying—
        springs with a laugh into living,
up from the earth, from dying.

Faustus, see
Margaret at her leaping, reaching hands;
she winds her wrists around
with blue and strikes her fists

against that tyrant who
        in a little time
will catch her at her skipping, in her sleep,
and stop all flying,
cover her with earth and down her bed
with small cold feathers from ungrieving skies.

COMING SUDDENLY
TO THE SEA

Coming suddenly to the sea in my twenty-eighth year,
to the mother of all things that breathe, of mussels and
      whales,
I could not see anything but sand at first
and burning bits of mother-of-pearl.
But this was the sea, terrible as a torch
which the winter sun had lit,
flaming in the blue and salt sea-air
under my twenty-eight year infant eyes.
And then I saw the spray smashing the rocks
and the angry gulls cutting the air,
the heads of fish and the hands of crabs on stones:
the carnivorous sea, sower of life,
battering a granite rock to make it a pebble—
love and pity needless as the ferny froth on its long smooth
      waves.
The sea, with its border of crinkly weed,
the inverted Atlantic of our unstable planet,
froze me into a circle of marble, sending the icy air out in
      lukewarm waves.
And so I brought home, as an emblem of that day
ending my long blind years, a fistful of blood-red weed in
      my hand.

A WINTER SONG

Desire has gone into his winter quarters
and all those other rioters that kept him company:
pleasures of meat and drink, sweat of wrestling,
dancing, keeping late hours, getting drunk;
those companions are scattered over the plains,
eat dry crusts, crack joints, read late, drink alone.

Old Desire has gone into his winter home
and all those young bucks, who used to keep him gay:
as the suns pleasures, and all the greenery
of the abundant grasses, where one lay
in an aproned lap; the pleasure of fingers
touching, and loving by a midnight flame.

King Desire has gone into his winter sleep
taking with him the revellers that made him brave:
rhythmic rounds rapped out in repeating praise,
the breath light with love, or heavy with delays;
the wave and the wind, delight beating the body,
that blew warm words upon a woman's face.

THE DEAD

After we knew that we were dead we sat down and cried a
    little, only we found that our eyes were now empty
    and we were without any feeling of sadness.
'We had it coming, it was bound to happen', said one.
'I am thinking of the future', said a lady beside him.
'There is no future', an old man affirmed.
'I'm glad', said one, looking back toward the earth. 'I'm free
    of it, I'm no longer one of them. I am glad'.
'So am I', someone echoed.
'So am I'.
'So am I', others repeated.
'So am I... So am I', the echo traveled along the plain and
    beyond. I did not know whether it was an echo, or
    whether others were there repeating the sound.
'So am I, so am I'... it went on, the whole valley and plain
    resounded.
I turned my eyes around to see, but there was only a grey
    transparency without end, and empty, that was like a
    wall before me. I could see as far as I wanted but I
    wanted to see nothing, and there was nothing.
One of the dead beside me stirred, and as if a memory had
    awakened him he said, 'They are always on edge
    down there. We were always on edge'.
'And there was also the fear of death', said a man of middle
    age.
'Someone there dies every day, every hour.
Think of the bird in the teeth of the hunter, beating its
    wings, crying out—
That was the way we were'. He fell into a deep silence. We
    all sat for a long time in silence.
Below us stretched the endless plain, and in the
    foreground, still near, the earth hung, like a sad town
    in a grey mist.
'There they sit, the beautiful women and the young men in
    their prime; time passes over them, and they shrivel in

ugliness, looking at one another in amazement. O, I am glad to be out of it. Glad to be rid of it'.

'But the worst is that even the innocent suffer', said a lady.

'They are all innocent', the old man muttered.

Then, raising his head, one poor skinflint beside me made a face like a devil who had done a good deed, and said, 'All this is important. I never worried about important things. The worst of it was, as I see it now... (he looked out across the plain into the grey distance without obstacle) 'was to be caught in a net that did not even exist'.

'When you are caught in a net', said the man of middle age, 'whether it exists or doesn't exist, it is still a net, and you are caught in it'.

'I don't even want to think of it', said the wizened man, as if losing interest;

'I remember', and here be bit his lip out of ancient habit, that even love was painful'.

And just as he said this, a dark cloud passed over us, and the earth was blotted out.

It brightened. But the figures beside me, and the earth that had formed a dark figure, receded, in no determinate direction, until I could see no longer. And then we were bathed in a morning light of sudden gladness. And there was nothing.

THEORY OF ART

In the wide circle of an eyeball
            at any moment
        the mind, or imagination, combines and recombines

windows and heads, a leaf and a cathedral,
            with unfailing unity,
        with a centre of interest, with an artist's iron will.

By the theory of optics, this *techne* is
            arrangement for
        the maximum of comprehension, to get in most of
                                    [a world—

miniscule cars at a distance and one's tree-sized finger
            perfectly fitted
        in the eyeball. And then you ask, 'What does it mean?'

They say 'the artist already tells you,
            and he does not know',
        since there is more in this than meets the eye, and
                                    [comes

from 'the greatest distance'. His centre of interest
            is crossroads of the world:
        where in the round, as in an eyeball, we must stand,

a real thing, the human edifice, or shrink
            unmetamorphosed
        back into the empty eyepits of the skull.

'The poem is vision'—but think of that diagram
            of light coming to focus
        from all quarters, to the miniature in a pupil—

the whole world, there in compendium, all
            its huge fragments
        a silent landscape, in the perfect O of the eye!

MIDNIGHT TRAIN

Falling pell-mell in a torrent past my eyes
telegraph posts and homes
run into the infinite bag of night,
the past behind us,
in which enclosed, as from a nightmare
we have hidden within our artifice of train,
the capsule, in which all objects seem both real and whole.
But I would break through and escape from this lie
and face the night of which I am impatient, yet afraid
I wish and wait for the sun to rise in blood
to halt the falling trees and homes,
stand all things again on their roots
and make the world turn in a great horizontal wheel,
or a road splayed up the mountain like a hand on fire.

THE VIGIL

I remember how my cat
Would come back cold and wet
Having sat, all night,
Without a hope he'd get
For all his holy care
A stroke of any fur.

So, thinking of her
In this bad weather,
And how saint, poet, civet,
All rained on skin and feather,
Suffer the same gnawing pain
Under roof, dome, or privet,

But yet do not resign,
Nay, do not resign—
Having seen the macaw,
Ostrich, and stinking crow,
Those loveless beasts, and their prey—
I raise my blood-drained face
To curse, as if to pray:

For this sunless place,
Made kinful by such cold,
Made noble, to be loved,
Takes what she will not take,
Gives what she cannot give,
And all the ecstatic beasts
One vigil keep, and live.

SPACES

The seven stars
of the Great Wain
hang in the sky
a million light years
one from another
and from me, but I
gather the seven together
who could never know
me or one another
but for my human eye.

MARRIAGE

Something in man delights
    in order and kindliness
    though the gods deny him.
Our fingers touching say this
    and the children sleeping
    in your untouched loins.

Tomorrow we join in marriage
    with ring and sweet song
    and the tears of the old.
When we die our dusts scatter;
    but where we have loved so
    no gods need recall.

PHAINETAI MOI...
(FROM SAPPHO)

Ah, but he's a lucky one, whoever he may be
    who sits by your side taking from your mouth
the honey-tongued syllables, while he gives back
    love to your white ears,

and hears your love-making laughter that so quick
    can fill my heart with wildness and excitement
that when I just look at you, all my words
    break up in my throat

and I'm just dumb before you, standing there,
    when suddenly a fire tears through my body
so that I cannot see a thing, and all my senses
    whirl in my ears,

then the sweat stands out on me, and a shaking
    takes hold of me, till I grow pale green
like grass, and like one dying I seem to
    fall to the ground.

THE CREATIVE ELEMENT

The love I have in me comes rising in great waves
        tossed at your mighty
small magnificent body, the floss of it
        a heavy foam, tossed
at your belly and shoulders till it overwhelms
        you, I feel it overwhelms you,
most beautifully, and makes an ocean around you.

Kiss me, kiss me now in this element! This
        is what they say started things,
this is how they created whales and things
        rolling it in a sea of storm,
overwhelmed and swirling in the fertile fury
        when the gods took chaos in hand.

LOVER TO LOVER

Desire that was wordless
for fear of each other
softly was spoken
louder than words:
body to body
diphthonged together
we know what a rhyme is,
a mouth to a mouth.
There was never a syllable
wasted on air,
we rocked to a rhythm
a thought laid bare,
and lie in a sleep now,
the world for a cradle,
silently spoken
and pious as prayer.

FROM CATULLUS

Let us live, my Lesbia, let us love!
And weigh the muttering of crabbed old men
as dust, against this one reflection:
Suns can set, and they can return,
but we, once our short light has ended,
in long perpetual night must sleep.

KOSMOS: THE GREEK WORLD
(FOR MICHAEL LEKAKIS)

One day man opened his eyes and the sun blew
over his wet eyeballs a coloured flower—
kosmos of combed fields
      and valleys where cattle grazed;
the hills folded in equations, and streams
bubbled mathematically to the sea; even the sea
strident, went silent,
      counted to ten and reined in;
and thunder gulped its peal.
    What memory of pain
he then denied, fought, shut his eyes to,
      or reconciled,
to make that intellectual gain! But he did.
It may be he mastered himself just then; or maybe
it was the blue Mediterranean dazed him
to think death is gay.
    Yet he found everything to praise.
God rose on the face of the waters I think that day
and smiled, his first recognition to clay.

R.I.P.

How do you think we'll rest
With tombstones on our chest?
I had rather recline
With your breast on mine,
    Love, on violets.

Or how shall we know peace
Broken piece by piece
In decay? I'd rather fret
Now for what I get
    From lips like these,

And leave nothing to wish
When we've become a dish
For the worms, my friend.
Leave them, hot heart, at end
    Cold cuts to finish.

NO ANSWER

A woodpecker knocked on my skeleton
   And found it very hollow
      And very thin
    Where all my aching marrow
      And blood had been.
Then he gave a rap and hopped
   To the crown at the top.

'Knock-knock! Who's there?' he spelled.
   'Tis I,' my soul replied.
      Then he with skill
    Hopped down and looked inside,
      Cleaning his bill
On my nose (or where it once was)
   With a wink and a pause.

'Ho ho!' said he. 'What's this? Are you there'?
   He cocked his head and clicked.
      'How's tricks, mon cher?
I see you've been cleaned and picked
      Something rare.
But can you hear it still in that box
   When your knees knock?

Ha ha!—in that box, when your knees knock'!
   I looked at him through my jaws
      And my empty eye,
    And got angry, and I was
      About to reply—
When he saw an apple tree
   And whistled away.

A CRACKER JACK

If you and I ceased to exist, my dear,
      and all other ghosts,
would the Manifold of Space and Time
      collapse in its cupboards?

Would the quivering fiction of being
      Joe, Paul, Patsy, May
be folded up like their Snakes and Ladders
      and be laid away?

As if we had not been? Not only 'as if'
      but as it is.
Nature destroys itself: we are and are not.
      Are now like this,

then never have been, when we cannot remember
      and no one is there to see
where shadfly swarms go after rainstorms
      or flies in a laboratory.

Our summer of strongest sunlight recalls
      the greatest sadness;
and the quiet contemplation of our extinction
      is called beauty, dearest.

OLD SONG

Since nothing so much is
as the present kiss
don't let an old kiss
so disconcert you,
but know it is no crime
to give a new kiss time
and reason to convert you.

The first you ever had
was an eternal lad
whose smile was very May
no other mouth replaces,
but this today has an October way
to harvest his embraces.

Loves are the fruits of time
different and the same
the perfect and imperfect,
and in the body's branches
where old kisses hang
and sweet birds sang
the wind fills his paunches.

And any kiss at all
is present after all
for now is all we have
now when we want them,
so grant your kisses leave
to give and to receive
nor waste your lips to count them.

DIVINE TOUCHES

Toiling with the white smoke of your body,
wreathed in the dark smoke of carnality,
I was whirled and turned into a feather of poppy
sleepily floating over distant people.
Now awake and alone
        I walk in the rain-soft night
borne still on that contemplation.
We become selfless by common living,
drowned in loud vision or in sound,
but what we are alone, or in love, is the risen self
        that gains from every birth or death
and walks out over the corpse of the flesh.

TAKING SHAPE

Taking shape
      (wings)
           of pigeons

make a temporary, a true
         forever continued
             perfection!

So everywhere
         whatever moves, whatever settles
rises on feet, or wings
         takes its shape;
ungrace is its undoing,
         a fear to fall,
            defection;

so consonants close
         (wings!) in a whorl
            of vowels—

the same
         and different
birds in other trees.

A SHORT SPEECH

Because they do not last,
        are they less a delight?
A lifetime itself is not a very long time,
and not a work of art either;
        but who would turn from it, the living of it,
            on that account?
We hang on as long as we can
        and hate to think how quick it flies.
And as for art, that's very long
        —at least we used to think so,
yet Chaucer says
        'al shal passe that men prose or ryme,
        take every man his turn, as for his tyme...'
And where are Sappho's best
        short-lived lines? Where are Abelard's songs?
What is most like true art
        looks as if it might not last,
looks as high and split-second beautiful
        as that quiver of your lips was...
And then, maybe it will last forever, who knows?

THE TOLERANT TREES

Some conspiracy of silence among the trees
      makes the young birds secret,
or laughing at our infirmities
        in birdlike fashion, they titter in feathers;
    but the uncondescending trees,
too wise to speak against us, against streamlining,
        against new fashions in uniforms and clothes,
wear always the same drab leaves,
      preserve a Sachem silence
toward our puberty rites of golf and war.

EMILY DICKINSON

I saw an oak tree in a pot,
    It was a very pretty thing:
Its branches had been often cut
    So that it kept its tiny plot.

The narrow body twisted up
    And glistened in the frightening sun;
Two feet of stem inside a cup—
    And yet an oak from root to top.

Nature is great in filling space
    Tight as an atom with desire,
But for a tree a room's no place;
    To put it there was a disgrace.

THE GREAT AS IF

If I die, love,
(as I must)
it is as if I had not been;

and for me, then,
this world
will be as if it had not been.

But who is less unreal?
You too will die,
we must all die, as if we had not been.

What, then, was this life?
Where was this world—
when all will be as if it had not been?

from

EN MÉXICO
(1958)

Language. Silence is
        also a language.
When there is no order in heaven,
we make what we make
by luck, or strength,
or the composition of desire.
Power grows
        like vegetation.
There are no preferences under heaven.
And I do not know why a leaf should of less worth
                than a Vatican
or why builders care;
but the mathematical stones recite their logic
of cruelty and despair:
we arose to gratify the reason
shaping the empty air.

How the temple came out of the heart of cruelty
and out of the jungle the singing birds!

That it should come into being out of nothing.
(Grass... bird... machine and metal,
    that they should come into being.)
Man, come to shape out of smoking matter,
    out of male secretion in the womb, take form.
All things, all bodies:
    that they should come out of nothing,
rise, as projectiles out of rock,
with spicules, with eyes, limbs,
with objects, accoutrements, skills,
amid an abundance of flora and fauna,
each to itself all—
in a jungle devouring graves.

So praise the glory of the green jungle
with all its terrible thunder;
praise death and generation
and the embracement of lovers under all skies.
Praise frost and thaw, and the congealing of elements,
or their prismatic flow;
        praise the disposition of ferns,
and the erection of great trees.
Praise hovels and giant domes
and the ant's most secular mound.
Between cathedral spires
and the plum tree's pleasantness
there is no distinction.
Praise these.

All the green blanketing the hills,
the braided streams,
and the brown sands bleaching;
horses with heads akimbo,
small lambs that leap
children with huge eyes,
and lovers shy in their look:
praise these to the bewildering heavens,
knowing no other tongue
but praise.

There were women washing
        by the edge of a stream, white
laundry on the hedge,
the hard cobbles and knuckles red.
I have looked through glass at the dividing process
and the war of germs:
after the passion and the split of creation
                (foreshadowing death),
the work of women by a crystal stream.

Stars I have never seen before, in the southern sky,
and clouds the colour of roses, of brown trees,
and the *copa de oro* when sun sets
                              in the far sky.
I have counted the new constellations
and gazed at the Great Way:
              there is no end to creation.
Cost what it may,
the petals of the infinite flower
          and time loves their sweet bouquet.

Someday we shall come again to the poem
as mysterious as these trees,
                          of various texture,
leaves, bark, fruit
(the razor teeth so neatly arranged,
so clean the weathered root).
There is the art of formal repetition
and the art of singular form—lines clean
          as a wave-worn stone...

Study the ancient habits
of the most disorderly people.
Where did reason arise?
The science of cleanness—
fastidiousness in art?
Somewhere in this, the market, the church,
                      the commissary.
No matter how steamy the jungle,
small leaves are perfect in detail.
Order remains unimpaired
in man and in matter,
despite all poverty, insanity, and war—
                      the jungle, in its excesses.
From wherever you are, begin!

To the peak of Popocatepetl
seen in the liquid sky
            (as we came from Taxco)
cutting the air with white precision.

—

I go out
      on a whirling wind,
an explorer's cry in my ears.

Time, time,
      over the clouds,
stretches ahead.

The cumulus grows. The ocean heaves.

Below me, the patterned fields
      lie green, and brown, and red.
Desert and jungle
      around the fertile plain.

Mexico, there—lies simple and bare;
strange as life anywhere.

from

LAUGHING STALKS
(*1958*)

THE LAYMAN
TURNED CRITIC

Seeing an elephant, he sighed with bliss:
"What a wonderful nightingale this is !'

And of a mosquito he observed with a laugh,
"What a curious thing is this giraffe."

ONE WORLD

Not only are the asylums overcrowded
but ordinary life is becoming uncomfortable
what with the number of madmen running about.

Nor in our minds is everything as it should be:
unreasoned fears. rages, faces made in the mirror,
not to speak of cramps and boils, to warn us of it.

And if the political gunmen aren't mad, who is?
There is some discord in nature. I tell you, the atom's split
has ripped the universe, down to the bit fingernail.

JAMES REANEY'S DREAM
INSIDE A DREAM,
OR THE FREUDIAN WISH

I dreamed that my grandmother
gave birth to a grandfather clock
and out of the clock came my grandfather
and in his hand was my jock:
and I awoke out of this dream
and dreamed I was putting on my sock
when out of the sock came my grandmother
holding my grandfather's jock:
and I awoke out of this dream
and found myself in my socks
under the grandfather clock,
and in my hand was *my* jock!

IRVING LAYTON'S POEM
IN EARLY SPRING

My friends, the people are devouring each other.
They will finish me off soon
with a gorpeous icepick.

They are mephitic as fly dung on cherry-stones.

But these pregnant buds opening like your
        genitals,
Are beautiful, dear, and swollen with greatness
Like my poems.

RICH MAN'S PARADISE
(AFTER F. R. SCOTT)

Behold these happy children at the Laurentian spa
Playing the juke box and drinking Coca-Cola:
Yet they must return to Lagauchetière Street
    After this little treat
To waste their stunted, unprofitable lives
For the profit of the few, under what we persist in calling
    "The System of Free Enterprise".

SOUSTER'S LAMENT
(WRITTEN WITH IRVING LAYTON
AND OTHERS AT THE KIT-KAT)

The beer was fine, the long green bottles on the table,
The lights were dim, the rhythm of the band just right,
The floorshow was just over, the girls gone for a
                quick one upstairs—
I wondered, what will they have in store for me—
When I said to myself, how long can you go on kidding
                yourself
About the beer, and the whores, and the Men's Room
                            [behind you
But we went on drinking, because there were still two
                bottles left
And we had aching hearts, and had lips.

QUEBEC RELIGIOUS HOSPITAL
BY A. M. KLEIN

Scarp Aesculapian, promontorious embole,
Refluct and invert of populous teleopaths.
My youth's diagony, jejeune floraison,
I bow to you crutchless, in memory's name...
(unfinished)

CARMAN'S LAST HOME

In "Sunshine House" lived Mrs. King
Where Carman with a turquoise ring
Dangled the bell, and often stayed,
Talked and sang, and wept and prayed.

At "Moonshine" on a summer's day
They danced in sandals—the Delsarte way—
While Unitrianian silence made
Their sorrows one, their joys a shade.

In "Ghost House' stayed eternal Bliss
Melancholy, despite all this:
Sang of pure Love, and the Mystic One,
Wore his hair long, his tie undone.

They have passed on, and "Sunshine" too,
As all great luminaries do:
A Ryerson Chapbook contains the man
Of Vagabondia and the Pipes of Pan.

EUROPE WITHOUT BAEDEKER
BUT "WITH" POUND

"The cakeshops in the Nevsky" !!
...Now here's a copy of Fracastoro's *Syphilis*
and Heywood's *Mayden-head Well Lost*...

Envy? They say Addison found six fingers
on a hand in one of Veronese's best pictures
And Tasso, in a rage, they say, of envy
tore out the pages
      of Ariosto with his teeth.

Je t'ai vu dans "Les Parapluies" de Renoir
...like Van Eyck, did the heads magnificently
but failed with the simple apples.

One of a democracy
      of artists.

As for Usura,
see the portrait of Asher Wertheimer
      (by Sargent)
Museums, attics of civilization...

HELLCATS IN HEAVEN
(REPORT ON THE BOOK "CERBERUS")

François Villon read one half,
Ended with a bitter laugh:
"May you be hanged for this,"
He said, "It's awful stuff!"

Next to read was William Blake,
Said in a fit of coughing shakes:
"Will you build Jerusalem
With the boards of a jakes?"

Read it then Arthur Rimbaud,
Read it shuddering as though
He had tasted something foul;
Then bawled, "Merde—ça pue!"

Read it Maître Rabelais,
Laughed, but fell a-cursing too:
" 'Tis true I said *faictz ce que veut*—
But how could I know what you would do?"

TAR AND FEATHERS

Layton, we write our clabbered verses,
Yours a long catalogue of curses,
Mine one pure curse the song traverses—
And yet the fact's we both know what
We're cursing isn't worth a futt.
Old Ez advises "build a sewer"
When culture's gone into manure;
Mistaking his advice at times
We make a sewer of our rhymes.
Of course, the Montrealers' lives
Are dismal—they deserve their wives—
Of course the poems in the *Star*
Are worse than yours and mine, by far.
And Westmount's cultured smell is spoil
Refined from Point St. Charles's oil.
Sure what they read and what they think,
And say, gives off an awful stink.
The soda fountain "five-foot shelf"
Would have choked Gutenberg himself;
The stomach turns from what they feed
Their young, like sparrows, true indeed.
And yet, we itch to double-kill
What there is left half-living still.
Think of the mountain how it stands
And doesn't give a damn what cans,
Cupcakes and condoms people throw
Over its calm Shakespearean brow.
There will be time yet, mountains think,
To wash all cities down the sink.
That's how I'd like to stand at last.
If lust or inspiration last,
Here by the Fount of Youth, it's warm,
Coffee and pie need no reform,
The waitress makes quick verses come.
Teenagers crowd around the rack
Of sex and crime, but stay intact.

To pin-ball magic eyeballs roll,
The Farmby Program fills the soul,
Telling the folks how many cows
Were burned last night while chewing chows,
Who had a birthday, who ate hash
And died of piles in St. Eustache...
And shall we curse the cook who makes
The pink floss on the Pom-Pom cakes?
Or bend to mop the floor with poems
They'll hang to drip in all good homes?
Such choices still defeat our ends;
Its waste of time that passion spends,
For dead men all know something worse
Than still to be alive to curse!
The young are coming, whistling songs,
And we shall go like dinner gongs.
But Montreal will have its fleas
Though what you write "to teach and please"
Is swelling notes for Ph.D.'s.

The waitress asks me, "Something else, sir?"
"No, thanks. For this, no Bromo Seltzer.

REPLY TO ENVIOUS ARTHUR

Hail Coprophilia, muse of Layton, hail!
Doxy of Dudek skoal! who drop'st in pail
Thick streaming words and brownish lumps of rhyme—
Manure essential in this barren clime.
Where Saxon critics without guts or gall
Praise these thy sons but little, if at all!
Yet these are they who vindicate thy cause,
Who preach thy gospel and affirm thy laws:
Blest pair of poets. put on earth by thee
To sweat and strain and groan to set us free
From Anglo-philistine hypocrisy.
What shovelfuls of praise we ought to pay
These swart forerunners of an Augean day
Let us with candour, clangour, and no taste.
Make haste to proffer, oh make haste, make haste!
Layton shall how to flatter Layton teach,
And modest Dudek Dudek's, glories preach:
Layton shall tingle in Canadian air,
And echo answer *Dudek* everywhere;
In ev'ry quarterly and magazine
Their linked names in squibs and puffs be seen:
Letters to editors be filled with them,
And gratitude replace each critic's phlegm:
Repentant Wilson, Smith, MacLure, and Frye
Shall who can praise than, loudest longest try.
                    A. J. M. Smith, *The Canadian Forum*. May, 1957.

It's little cause, Arthur, you have to complain
That I, or that my friend, may sometimes gain
A cough, or even applause, when we appear
To shout into the the thick Canadian ear.
The nation being deaf to poetry, you know
We're heard in London or Lansing, but not in Sault.
But you lack recognition for your pains
In whispering over the last cold remains
Of your own talent, or for Scott and Klein.
So naturally you resent *our* doing fine.
Remember there were times when you yourself
Were not above impacting critic's pelf.
Before your first, best, gifts forsook you
Before you'd published any book you
Had old Professor Collin sing hosannas
To you, in this windy *White Savannahs*.
Some six years later, bringing out your thin
First volume—how you took the critics in!

Almost posthumously, it might be said,
Since as a poet you were good as dead:
News of the Phoenix—as if any news
You brought was ever novel to the Muse!
You scaped the country after this affair;
Then from a cloud, or from a college chair,
You wrote, in ignorance, of "traditions", "trends".
"The Cosmopolitan", "The Native"—nonsense without
    end.
At last, anthologizing others' wares,
Your own name grew on theirs, so it appears,
Till forc'd to publish or renounce your fame
You brought *A Sort of Ecstasy* out—a sort of lame
Last book, stuffed with discarded rhymes
That even our critics could not praise this time.
(Some of the poems were so little new
They came out of a 1928 Review;
And not a poem but was cribbed, 'tis said,
From Yeats, Pound, Auden, or the greater dead.)
The critics shook their heads, admired your skill
In writing nothing, and yet publishing still.
Ah well, you've always aimed at verse, we know.
So fine, by dint of labour labour would not show;
But in your own smooth lines, for lack of pith,
Only the labour shines—no genius, Smith!
Give over, then; and give up envy, man;
Let others win applause, or steal renown.
There's little glory, even for men like us,
Who've genius without labour, without fuss.*

---

* It may surprise some readers to learn that I am and always have been an admirer
of A.J.M, Smith's poetry. This kind of duel among poets is largely an exercise in
poetic skills, and I am sure that Smith's couplets were written in the same spirit.
One does smart, of course, under the snap of wit, and I was provoked. But later I
wrote a newspaper piece under the title 'A.J.M. Smith, Aesthetic Master of Ca-
nadian Poetry." L.D.

THE RACE

Pine trees that grow 200 feet in the air
and have no green but a bunched Christmas tree
            at the top

have done it through competition
with other trees,
like the armaments race,
            or skyscraper cities,

each trying to get the light from the other,
until all are too far from the earth
to get enough juice,
and suck it a half-mile up
            for a mere living.

SEQUEL TO BROWNING'S "LAST DUCHESS"

There he stands now, my lord, done in the best bronze:
I'd have no other; stands, for all his marbles
Stowed in the scullery. A four-months I worried
Blind Ambrogio for that likeness, just that look,
As though he were to say, "You know your master!"

Was it the middle of winter, I first saw him?
Prim, like those stiff dolls on a wire at a fair,
Or sparrows marking the snow—alert and smiling;
Not that smile, another, a twist at the edge
As though a love-jest was to drop. The gesture
Won me: a usurer's promise. Then these walls closed;
They've said, "a rose shut in a black volume—"
Or "one of your saints," the barred barbarous script
Grilling me about the sides with its cursed *Amen.*

Silence. He'd a way with him, of holding no parley
With complainers: as when he'd rough-spoke peasants
Scored in the tongue for saying once too often
He claimed some service. O, not unkindly!
Let them walk tongueless in his grounds after
At petty wages! I have known such silence
You'd think no sea could be so great and empty.

But he, even that night, was gay, and pleasant:
As was his habit, mounting the staircase, bid me
Stand again before his relict, the late dead duchess
Who smiles now in our daylight—I've bit lip
To the sweet blood looking on her—but not then!
For then I turned smiling, as she would smile,
He pulled the curtain, and I stood waiting
In the still air for the good drop to rise
To his heart and work, Oh, his look;
His look had no triumph, I have kept that look
Where only I can draw the curtain. Here
Let him stand for master, I would have him so,
Where he may see his duchess rule Ferrara,
And post to Trier, seals for the Emperor's self!

THE PROGRESS OF SATIRE
(FOR F.R. SCOTT AND A.J.M. SMITH)

Reading a dead poet
Who complained in his time
Against bad laws, bad manners,
And bad weather in bad rhyme,

I thought how glad he'd be
To be living in our time
To damn worse laws, worse manners.
And worse weather, in worse rhyme.

DON'T TALK

Lovers have no need to talk

After the act he said
thank you
and thus offended

He should have boasted rather
of his gift
    or said nothing

If you did this for sixteen hours
the perfect lover said
I would let you sleep for eight

So don't talk

from

ATLANTIS
(1967)

How seagulls know what they are!

So to be, whatever you are —
            a white bird,
                        a man with a blue guitar.
But there is room for more, more.

It is the part of us
not yet finished as seagull or man

that worries us at the pit of creation,

hanging over cliffs, drowning,
                        or lifted in flight

to new states of being, asking always what we are.

Speaking of coral, the white whirling wave
behind the ship
is like a Japanese painting of a wave.

It is not the painting that is like a wave
but the wave like a real painting—
as exact, as detailed, as white and delicate,
made of many tiny hands, of drops, of lacing lines,
a continuous flocculation of white light
that is unlike mere water as a Rembrandt is unlike mere
                                                [paint.

That nature is the prime artist does not mean that
                        all nature is art.
The means are wasteful, but the occasional fragment
may be a masterpiece, a poem, or even a man.

Today we passed over Atlantis,
                    which is our true home.
We live in exile
waiting for that world to come.

Here nothing is real, only a few
                    actions, or words,
bits of Atlantis, are real.

I do not love my fellow men
                    but only citizens of Atlantis,
or those who have a portion
of the elements that make it real.

———

Marble is the cross-section of a cloud.
What, then, if the forms we know
                    are sections of a full body
whose dimensions are timeless
                    and bodiless, like poems,
whose unseen dimension is mind?

I want to learn how we can take life seriously,
        without afflatus, without rhetoric;
to see something like a natural ritual,
        maybe an epic mode unrevealed,
in the everyday round of affairs.

———

Marina is gone to Abruzzi
                    for a wedding

She will be all in white
                    like a small ship
trailing a veil.

          Her bands will hold flowers,
          she will drink wine,
                    break bread.

And she will be as beautiful
                    as I have always dreamed she was.

I am tired of people who come gaping at churches.
In the middle of High Mass
                    on Easter morning
they gape at the dome, while others pray with their
                                        [eyes down.

Not to be with them, I will pray for this once.

The church is merely a structure
to contain the emotions of those who feel.
It is sometimes a work of art for those who do.

I have seen an early drawing of Jesus
                    sitting on a hill, reading a book.
Beyond all the incense and sulphur
                    he sits in meditation still,
a man who died for love.

And so much the memory of it is real
          that where love is, they say, he is risen.

There are too many people. Of course there are too
                              [many people.
But they haven't ruined the world.
They only make it more difficult to survive
    (in ten years, or a hundred, we may need more men).
The point is not to stop breathing
            but to make room for more.

Even the dirt is necessary.
It's some kind of beauty in ruin,
                like a falling rose.
Even new dirt contributes to beauty,
    it is what we have to do, if we want to live.

But for any people, their life is visible
            in the kind of beauty they create.

In a way, it's one vast slum,
                the world.
Or a rich garbage dump
on which gaudy flowers and delicate pinks
                sprout, clamber, float;

a ghostly beauty rising over decay

on tip-toe stems, hardly touching the earth,
        points of transparent, watery dew.

When the girl said she hated lizards
                                at Pompei
I thought: It's all in the family, you know,
                we are all lizards.

If you loved all of it, you would also love lizards.
It's only a part of yourself you hate.

Look at your hand!

—

And the people, with their doors in the narrow streets,
                                with their bimbi, and bags,
what have they to do with Empires,
                or art, or a Renaissance of power?

They are the eternal soil,
                the raw matter of mankind.

To understand their little corner shrines
remember that it was Jesus
who first taught us to think of the poor and
                to love them.

—

Time is the illusion
that makes all existence null and void
                and cleaves to what is living still.

So Rome is Khrushchev, America.
What was once the state is now a machine.
And the dead artists who painted walls
                are cutting flowers on Italian glass.
Nothing is lost, the world is fuller than it ever was.
What is cut down in one quarter
is probably somewhere that much more alive.
And if the whole world should perish,
do you think the powers that made us would fold up
                                [and die?

How the unreal hours pass by,
                              soon forgotten!
Where there is no ecstasy there is no reality.
That's why we slaver for the mere crust of it.

I remember the little man singing "Marutsa"
on the ship, a little red-faced Italian
with a permanent smile,
      weaving and shutting his eyes, to sing and dream:
a moment of time,
but there isn't a detail I have forgotten.

All great beauty
shows the triumph of life
                  floating on a sea of storm,
a glory that must end in sighs.
At the height of great music
            (whether of Puccini or Bach)

one forgets the meaning, the lovers,
            the loss, even one's own tragedy, even God—
only to hear a sound
beyond all meaning, beyond art,
            a whiteness only, where all meanings start.

I believe that the poem has a generative form
                  like coral or hurricane.
Every white detail must be employed.

Looking at the cold sculptures
                  in the very cold museum
I saw a work of art walking about.

Her hair was brown and tumbling,
            her stockings down to her calves
                              in a tight line.

She made the place warm
            with one gleam of her smile.

The infinite clarity when it began
                              (if it began)

divided itself in space and time
            an infinite world of infinite worlds.

Their folding together in love, and friction in pain,
                        unseals like mica
the leaves of quality on every hand.

But I have been in a marine aquarium and I have seen
                LOLIGO VULGARIS
                TRACHINUS ARANEUS
                SCORPAENA SCROFA
                SCYLLARIDES
                ANEMONIA SULCATA
                ASTEROIDES CALYCULARIS
                MAJA SQUINADO
                MUSTELLUS LAEVIS
                THALASSOCHELIS CARETTA
                TRIGLA CORAX
                TRYGON VIOLACEA
                HYPPOCAMPUS BREVIROSTRIS
                SPIROGRAPHIS SPALANZANII
                ACTINIA CARI
                MURAENA HELENA
                SYNGNATUS ACUS
                RETEPORA MEDITERRANEA
                PELAGIA NOCTILUCA
                PARAMURICEA CHAMALEON

Of a very graceful undulant movement
                of a pale white colour
                        with translucent fins

Fish that lie buried in the sand, on the sea bottom,
                with only their eyes peering out

Or long and thin as a pencil
                        flexible in movement

Or absurd, barnacled, monstrous bulldogs of the deep,
                    and sea-spiders of gigantic size.

Red flowers of the sea
                    (or orange coloured)
          like carnations, like broken pieces of pomegranate

(I too was once a fish
I rubbed myself on the sea bottom, leaping gracefully
                    A large fish, about two feet long)

There was one like a great sturgeon
                    constantly moving and twisting its muscular body

And a fish with tentacles under the fins
                    on which it walks on the sea floor!
It has a blue fin, that opens when it swims
And speckled fish, too, with the eyes of snakes
          at the bottom of the sea, their heads gently bobbing

And an Octopus
with saucer-like suckers, a paunchy body,
     huge eyes on great mounds,
blowing out of intestinal tubes,
                    coiling the tips of his tentacles like a seashell.

He looked intelligent
Maybe he is intelligent, I thought, like a poet
                    or a philosopher
who understands, but cannot act to circumvent clever men.

The octopus opened his magnificent umbrella,
pushed the belly forward, and bumped into a sleeping fellow
Then he went behind a pilaster
                    becaue I had been watching him too long.

A magnificent creature.

And I saw beautiful tiny sea-horses
                    with a fin on the back
                              vibrating like a little wheel

And a ghostly shrimp six inches long
                              light pink and white
and graceful as a star, or the new moon

And a whorl of delicate white toothpicks
And brown stems, with white strings like Chinese
                bean-sprouts, long and graceful.

And I saw a wonderful turtle.

But I have seen fish, turtle, octopus, with dead eyes
              looking out at the world.
What is life doing? waiting for something to come?
Are we all stepping-stones to something still unknown?
Is man, when he is glad, when he is in love or enthralled
              at last getting a glimpse of it?
Are the birds? Are the swift fish?

(Or perhaps they know they are captive. Who can tell,
even a fish may know when it is not at home.)

Then I saw a thin, thin thing
undistinguishable from a twig (just a few inches long)
but on close inspection very beautiful.

Since he has disguised himself to look so unremarkable,
              for whom does he keep that secret form?

There was a light green jelly
              PHYSOPHORA HYDROSTATICA
And a kind of huge one-foot-long paramecium
              PYROSOMA GIGANTEUM

And a thread-like plant with fragile white hair
(They say the chromosomes are such a thing of diminutive
              size, the whole life contained in their genes!)

And a coral that was a true artistic design
              made by a growing plant—
                      a Persian decorative motif.

And many other intelligent plants, animals, and fish.

No matter how it glitters, how it shines,
                                    it will vanish.
The street vendors, the Partenope, the trees
                will vanish.
The pink and lemon walls, the grey, the dark designs
will fade like chalk in a pale snowy light
        and leave only memory, tracings in a dream.
And we will discover other cities with the same
                beauty, looking for the one true
and lasting city, that may never be.

                        ⌐

In the Villa Borghese gardens, high and beautiful trees
                seem to vanish into the blue.
The sun sits like a bird
        somewhere in those branches.

I believe the purpose of all being
is to be luminous and reaching like these trees—
true to the character of beauty
        that moves and is whatever moves.

                        ⌐

All we are looking for, so distant,
                so difficult, so near...
in each, the least, the same, chaos and blind chance
                —out of which nothing, or something,
                        or some great good may come.

The gods are not behind it all, they are in front of it.
They do not make things happen.
                They find it enough to approve.

                        ⌐

The days, the streets, the people,
                    are an unstable means, a bridge
to what is yet to be, or else can never be entire—

that grows, and moves, like clouds
                    piling over the world and time,
in the cloud-white of marble
                    or an acropolis of words.

Certainly this cross-section of an instant
                    is not all the world there is.

—

What is it that a poet knows
                    that tells him—'this is real'?

Some revelation, a gift of sight,
granted through an effort of the mind—
                    of infinite delight.

All the time I have been writing on the very edge of
                    [knowledge,
heard the real world whispering
                    with an indistinct and liquid rustling—
as if to free, at last, an inextricable meaning!
Sought for words simpler, smoother, more clean than any,
                    only to clear the air
of an unnecessary obstruction...

Not because I wanted to meddle with the unknown
                    (I do not believe for a moment that it can be done),
but because the visible world seemed to be waiting,
                    as it always is,
somehow, to be revealed.

Whoever has once heard that music, in that quiet light,
knows what he has to say, over again and over.

—

In the church which is already music (Notre Dame),
wrapped in many coats against the grim cold,
                    we heard the Requiem of Brahms.
The old cathedral seemed to shake
        so that we feared for the glass in the precious windows
when the music of the sopranos and the bass
        combined in solemn chorus
                    with strings, flutes, and brass.
And when the Requiem was ended,
                why did no one applaud?
Because to praise men is foolish who have praised God.
There is something more than man, we all know it,
                that like a Requiem silences human applause.

—

I met a very pleasant German girl, with her parents,
        on a visit to Paris for a few days.
We talked over the table. I walked her home.
She expressed herself with difficulty in English.
Who thinks more of Auschwitz, she or I?

Who visits the Louvre?
    Or who owns the Parthenon frieze?

The sea belongs to whoever sits by the shore.

—

A white new moon
            floated along the light blue sky.
I opened my mouth and
saw a beautiful girl walking with a tall black boy
                        holding hands.
They went that-a-way!

(The moon, also, vanished
                    over the choppy rooftops of Paris.)

And I went to hear Menuhin,
                    maybe another way
out of the Metro, into an Alhambra of sound.

But caught by a continuous thread
    making an intricate design, that covered heaven,
ended bemused, entangled, in mid-air.

And fell back into Montmartre
among the gridirons and three-cornered squares
the café bars and dim hotels
                    and sad soliciting girls
(and a man throwing up his guts on the sidewalk
            after a good time).

Yet paradise is here or it is nowhere...
In streets of night and morning,
and men broken by labour,
and the mountainous loom of daylight
                        filling the dark night.

Here or nowhere,
among the people empty of light.

Mind is real—it is all we know—
                    and matter merely a conception.
What is death, but an unimportant transfer, a denudation?
Think of yourself as an eternal existence
undergoing this fiction
                    for a purpose—
no doubt, to see what you will do with it!
If you like, a creative experiment.
There is no reality, here,
Whatever there is, we make it.

Whatever it is, since there will be others after us
                    (by some necessity),
it is important that they should not be lost;
that we discover, add to, do whatever helps
                                        to enlighten them,

to find, in the initial darkness,
            —what, if not the final reality?

＊

Do the gods stand behind the shadow world
and say, find us, imitate us
                recreate us without seeing us?
No, it is we who create the gods
and tell them to perfect us,
                to recreate us, in their image.

While behind the gods there is something further still
                    that shines, gleaming and unimaginable,
like a beautiful secret, gift-wrapped in silence.

＊

Time floats like an island
                     in the sea of being.
We must study
its birds and flowers as language
               that tells us our past and future.
For there is no other knowledge.

Think of the idiots who want a "vision",
               having the sun-blasted world before their eyes.
It has been given!

We have only to read the signs.
What would it be to me if I heard voices
                     (I hear your voice);
What if I saw a spirit
                     (when I see your face)?
It is impossible not to read the signs.
The very eyesight speaks, and the ear sees,
while all the visionaries grope in the dark.

My favourite reading place in Paris
                     was a small park
by Saint-Julien-le-Pauvre
with the old church at the back
               and the cathedral in front,

the traffic passing by, and children at play
               (new ones asleep in their mothers' arms),
and languid lovers on the shady seats, holding hands.

A beautiful woman on a bench
               with a line of cars behind her.
The hedge, the fence, the trees
                     like a poem on a page.

But actually the trees speak an older meaning:
I look at the wandering trunks, the leaves,
               the dark serenity of silence
that no one in the city sees.

Happy the man who has some world he loves,
                            that he can call his own,
to which he can return.

Like the waitress in the café
                hugging her mug of café-au-lait,
to whom the streets belong, the street markets, the shops,
                                            [the men
            and life is a round of genial affairs.

Without it there is no *beau voyage*,
                        only homelessness,
a world of strangeness that is not a place.

Venus, the love that ennobles the body.
Apollo in the breathing stone.

They now exist in modern Paris,
                    city of barmen and bistros,
of bateaux mouches and métro—
                        so soon to be extinguished.
Seen for a moment, like a carnival of fireworks,
            to 'Ohs' and 'Ahs' of surprise,
                        the glittering appearances,
they vanish, leaving some paintings—
        "Paris as Seen by the Masters",
                        poems, or music,
caught in the amber of art
like dead flies, with twigs and leaves around them.

From the High Renaissance to the nineteenth century
painting adjusted its forms
                    (beginning with myth and divinity)
until it had found the actual, real,
in the immediate moment of living.

But a moment is brief.

And no sooner had they found it
than the mystery vanished in formal vision,
                    a spray of lights, or a cloud of shadows,
or just paint flashing across a screen.

Now they are far away and more remote than ever
                    from the sensual present.
And they have gone to the secret processes
                                of nature,
that makes form, out of whirling chaos, and energy,
the place of the unborn, titanic powers.

                    ━

The soil of England, June flowers
                    in the bright sun,
daisies and purple vetch,
and soft sheep nibbling in the shade.

Ramshackle huts in the allotments,
                    old country homes by the road.
Even the weeds are domestic on this billowing land
        of soft contours, small valleys, brackish streams,
and lawns like one continuous golf course.

                    ━

Have you seen the weeping beech
        hanging like a green pavilion?
Or the tulip tree
        reaching up to heaven?

Have you seen the cedar?
The kakee tree, the gingko, the lobed sassafras
          —have you inhaled their fragrance

The glistening leaf of the strong oak, suber,
      the slender white birch,
            the dappled maple,
the tough sticky pine, swelling with rosin?
Have you sat on the moss among the brown cones?
Have you seen the contours of the leaves?
Or listened to the silence in their shadows,
        or the rush in high winds?

I have gone to the green pavilion of morning
        and watched the dahlia open her eye.
I have seen the violets breathe in the blue light
        under pendent leaves.

—

Everything that passes is semblance for a day —
      the dirty Thames (dirtiest of rivers)
             with all that it bears —
and the few of us look back through time
      seeing the Titians, churches, the Roman shields
and catch for a moment a glimpse of pattern
      — O not the real, not substance
        but a hint of sequence —
that others, caught in time,
      pitched from moment to moment, falling,
may find an instruction, a hope,
      a breath of encouragement...
But how could they cease
their watery progress to listen, to think of the emptiness
that still surrounds us, the shreds of our meaning,
in the precipitate rush of existence?

Ah, Wyndham!
Cophetua may still rhapsodize
                            but at the Tate
I did not find Ezra, where he used to hang
                    almost life-size.

The beard replaces the necktie,
            the pub gives way to the espresso bar.

And poetry is the fruit of experience!
The present is always present!
                            Ha! Ha!
All you've got to do is be there to enjoy it.

The dead don't care — they're neither here nor there.
            Something keeps the world always full,
                            like a daily newspaper.
An atomic ticker-tape?
                Ghost writers

In a corner of a London museum
I saw the ballet shoes and feather-white dress of Pavlova
                    in which she danced The Swan,

with old clothes, torn gloves, and bits of broken glass
                    from those times.

And Adelina Patti's tiara —
            a triumph in La Sonnambula —
buried in a downstairs room.

—

Ilex Aquifolium, the pale-fringed holly.
The Strelitzia like a tropical bird,
          the hanging lamp of the purple fuchsia.
The rose Spiraea and the royal lily.
(And birds come to eat from your hand—
                    would you want to harm them?)

Gleditschia   Dietes   Regal Lily

Not that the poem doesn't have a meaning.
          It's what holds the thing together,
an invisible ghost.

I have seen the parts of a flower
          floating, detached from the stem,
yet knowing somehow what to do.
Growing, drinking in rain.

Callamandra   Zantedeschia   Gloriosa

And an orange tree, with dozens of fruits

—

This is all new to me.

The half of a moon.
The sound of feet.

Should I ask that tree?
          Listen with my ear to the ground?
Study a flower for a sign?

I will take it all in and wait
          until like a Univac
I suddenly throw up the sum.

This will be always true, as it is now (as all we do),
and each living thing an enameled bird
                    of paradise.

———

I saw a graveyard where the stones had been ranged
                along the side as a low wall,
while the space itself was turned into a children's
            playground.
We are always trampling on the bones of the dead.

It all comes down to this life of ours
of which you have the pieces
                    right in your hands.

———

In the daylight of departure from the shores of light,

the sea was a white burning cloud all afternoon.

Locks hanging over the counterpane
                    or grapes spilling
out of the bright horn.

"Light."

Only in the reflection of portholes
                            gulls
flash across mirror, a dumb sequence.

The sea as an escritoire.
                That pale blue
          and violet
                  heaven.

Like dreams before they begin, a tunnel
            at the end of which a blue grotto,
silently set with shrubs, shines.

Silence, in the glass light of so much meaning
it looks like indifference, and purpose so large
            the details are left to chance.

What I think when I am alone

of the sea, the road of adventure
        — what the soul sees between two lives. Hearing
                                      [only

the plaintive seagull's infant cry.

We go into darkness, into deeper darkness,
                 where all embryos are shattered.

An emptiness, void of meaning,
                  a signless nil
cancelling out all mathematics.

The great zero of nature, in which the little numbers flicker
               like a halftone of nazi crosses
without significance.

Concentration camp of souls.

With gas chambers and crematoria:
        "genocide" of all mankind and all animal species.

"All these must die" — by order
           of the Supreme Authority.

A scientific experiment.

There, somewhere, at the horizon
        you cannot tell the sea from the sky,
where the white cloud glimmers,

the only reality, in a sea of unreality,

out of that cloud come palaces, and domes,
                and marble capitals,
and carvings of ivory and gold—
                 Atlantis
shines invisible, in that eternal cloud.

I see my angel, flying over the water,
to the blue that's like a thin gas flame around the world.

Leave me, I said,
        spirit that rise above today and tomorrow.

Already I hear
        the creatures are laughing at my words.
No one understands. It does not interest them.

Even my anecdotes must fail.

Fragments of poetry that float on the water
        as common seaweed.
A bottle. A board.

How will I separate them
        from the drift of snow?
Or amanita, from the edible food?

Nothing—is always true.
In any crisis, it's the best thing to do.
Nothing—is what it comes to.
It's where we begin.
Nothing—is what we like to do.

Everything comes of nothing.
It "never faileth",
it is as good as charity—those who have nothing
        also have faith and hope.

Nothing is silent. Nothing is simple.
Nothing is left to chance!
Nothing is at the heart of mathematics,
        and number the nothing in all that is.

from

COLLECTED
POETRY

(*1971*)

LATE WINTER*

The sky is scrubbed clean,
        the chimneys stand like springtime sticks
growing out into a world done over.
A fresh lacquer of rain
        dries on the tree branches.

        But the sun is stony
on the houses, on walls of factory metal,
on the tops of buildings
        distinct as in a mortuary.
On the distant roofs it lies cold
like platinum, that the waste
        cotton clouds have polished.
Nature stiffens
        her water-tints in times like these,
makes morals out of her fairy-tales.

---

*   This section begins with eight early poems. L.D.

SKYSCRAPER WINDOW

At the ice-bright window,
if you let the light
dazzle you with silver blisters from
the hump-backed cars, that crawl
aching, in rows
to a green light,
and if you look
down canyons, into distant boroughs
where at last they die like proboscidians
among the ivories and striated marbles
of St. James street,
you may wonder if history
ever knew, or would have been surprised;
if in the streets, the cries
and the coughing in corners,
and the falcons fluttering with blood-stained beaks
could have been foretold
for our pity and amazement,
and whether the nerves we learn by,
teeth, and veins, are tough enough,
and weaponed
to break alive into the green beyond.

WOMAN

These are poetry, which would be sung—
the budding genitals, the fearful phallus,
man's elemental organs as beautiful
as a geyser rising suddenly upward,
a wonder woman will always love.
Stroking the foam of violent hair
and bathing under the soft spray
beating up from masculine marble,
the virgin will become brown and ripe
her body radiating with tbe sun.
At her touch some irrepressible lad
like an eaglet under a dove's wing
will thresh with menace, and assault
her fears with infinite excitement.
Secret genitals—wonders to be sung!
And woman, if she support the storm
of that chaotic ocean rolling over
her world shattered by male strength,
if tasting the bowels of the earth
in their salt, malignant purity,
she return to love, and to man's cruelty
her whip of nature, asleep and weak—
her reward is to walk with sun-born women,
such as own the skies, and mother great birds.

TREE IN A STREET

Why will not that tree adapt itsclf to our tempo?
We have lopped off several branches,
cut her skin to the white bone,
run wires through her body and her loins,
yet she will not change.
Ignorant of traffic, of dynamos and steel,
as uncontemporary
as bloomers and bustles
she stands there like a green cliché.

THE MOUNTAINS

In streets, among the rocks of time and weather,
with the crisp noises around, and the surrounding voices,
hearing the steel of wheels repeatedly, like bayonets,
and the sound of guns from buildings, where the windows
icily shut suddenly like visors, and men are marching;

past the trucks stooped in rows like horses
with sacks thrown tenderly over their shoulders,
the hooded and silent heroes in garages—
I walk, though the frost-fire plays in my fingers
and my eyes are crying in this freezing weather.

And amazed, I hear a few anxious voices
rise extemporizing in the hoar-frost air,
singing, on this plateau, our latest position
high in the mountains, near the dividing line
where it is coldest, and the rocks are a parapet.

Yes, soon, the hills scaled, we shall look down
into bright greenery, valleys, and rivers
thinning into wheat-fields! And the cold air like water
will flow from us, while we gaze and gaze
at the low valleys, and the meandering rivers.

BUILDING A SKYSCRAPER

By the Street's noise muffled, the hammers
sock silently; a mittened hand
plucks concrete pieces from the ground,
throws them with a curse without a sound,
as automatic these men
building a skyscraper in the precincts of Wall street
work without being heard, without headlines, with only
a truckful of sand making rapids of applause.

Skyscrapers have their origins in the Stone Age.
Under the concrete feet of every hall,
under steel, this hammering must be done. So pausing for
                                    [the bow,
these partners, prototypes of mankind consider
the hole they have made, a place to open a pail, unwrap
                                    [paper
and eat ham, a cave this winter—but a bone-heap
of vapour and people next summer, a skyscraper.

And here is surprise and paradox; one of the boys
leaning on a handle sports a pipe, is no longer primitive:
the stem is silver, and a luxury of billows
expands from the bowl!
Now he folds on his belly over a steam-drill
and shakes like dead meat—but to him stones give way
and walls fall; he kicks them to hell and the crane,
makes room for a girder, for a small finger
to hold up an iron web in the air,
metallic bones hung in the velvet night,
and clothed with flesh, a hand between the moon and
    men's eyes.

The same man may rivet as well as work a drill,
may measure the dimensions, or draw a blueprint,
approve the designs and pay the bills:
but for a name and a number the same man
plans a city, and builds it, and writes it a religion.

We are identical in everything but words and clothes,
the track we took from the unequal springboard of the
[womb.

Tomorrow I will come and watch their progress
I know for certain that these digging men
nudging each other with their elbows, pushing the drill left,
scoop clay from under the rump of profit and finance.
Digging here and in the next street, today or tomorrow,
something will finally happen, a bank will sag,
a building sway like a fork on a prong;
with shouting and throwing from side to side, the houses
will fall into the diggers' arms. The Stone Age will be done.

And then, a colosseum will be made of the street,
sidewalks will become benches, and windows break with
[cheers.
We will praise "Men Working." They will be celebrated
more than millionaires, since without rich men
nations can run as well, or better, but not without these
[men.
And because they now work inaudibly, cursing behind a
[fence,
I know that someday, over the applause and clamour
of the crowd, will fall on every ear the workman's hammer.

PUERTO RICAN SIDE-STREET

Morning came at me like a flung snowball,
the light flaked out of a chalk-blue sky;
and I was walking down the dilapidated side-street
like a grasshopper in a field, just born;
all the rails and pails glistened and deceived me
with bunches of blue flowers and with silk of corn.

The yellow shades were mostly down, some up, some torn;
and I went looking into windows, into rooms,
looking for the breakfasters, and the cluttered dressers
and cracked walls; watching the black doorways and the
        dim
charred halls, for the baby carriages and the kids;
and as I walked, they came, like shots in a foreign film.

And then, in a blue window, lifted like a cross,
her legs straight, hair flat, and arms strung wide,
gazing out at the daylight out of coal-black
glassy eyes, I saw the twelve-year child—
a saint upon a stained-glass window—with her blue sash
                                    [dress
hanging on her, thinly, and her small face thin and faint.

As I passed looking at her eyes held far away,
she almost turned; but the sun suddenly came
from behind some chimney stack, and I went ahead:
the street blazed up again. The morning hour,
that made the ashes shine and the stones burst out in flame,
had shown me in her face the sad, dark human flower.

AT LAC EN CŒUR

1

What kind of honey does a bce get from a thistle?
A purple bomb, toxic
                with spears of language.

Hating pretentiousness,
            or the vanity of writing poems,
I sit for hours without a word.

The hidden bios, cosmos, works with his emotions
shaping things into multiform shapes of desire.

He never says a word
                nor even (perhaps) thinks a thought
but fits the liver under the beating heart
as the artist places his cove and tree,
                        feeling his way
                    to the complex unities.

We cross-section this work of love
                        when we think or talk.

2

Nothing is eternal. Not even the trees
though I gather that some are longer-lived than a man.

A whirling flashlight
                makes a permanent wheel.
Moving lights. We are a web.

Unity, out of motion and diversity,
            as real as atoms.

The blue sky turning pale green at the horizon,
only one streak of cloud
                beyond the birch leaves overhead.
The trees, cedar, some maple, and tattered pine,
below them the fern and smaller brush,

dead leaves, brown earth, rock
(a canoe on the still water makes a slapping sound)

And I sit, the ache in my bones receding,
            a thought breathing cold air—

shaping a world already made
                to a form that I require.

3

Since all things contemplate themselves
a mouse in a ditch
                observes itself,

in silence, slips underground
in solitude eats, twitches, curls and sleeps...

Does no one approve? No one care?
How can he exist—
                    alone?

A mouse goes without fear, alone, as if
            with love's eye upon it.

4

Cottages like Chinese lanterns
                shine in the soft dark
I breathe the moist night, by the lakeside

Fishes peer at our intrepid lights,
                ephemeral man-blown stars
in their familiar trees

The road is lit by a small lamp,
waving with my body's swing,
            rocked at the pelvis, to and fro,
as I pass, leaving the great
                shadows behind
and the green domes in the night.

5

Some men murder fishes, others kill quail
all for sport. The trees fall

like great sick animals, eaten by the saprophytes in their
                                                    [sides.

We have no time, to hate or mourn.
Love the arrowy fern, mean moss, and furry bee
enough to forgive all

fools out of despair
that, dying, cover fear
with laughter, guns, or game on a hook.

                              6

Alone in the forest
I hear the wind overhead,
          see the lake through the trees.

Several monsters are allayed.
I sit on a high rock, alone,
listening to the wind, looking through the pines.

In front of me a fir
sends up a central stalk
          with four pedicles around it

(only by keeping apart from the others
                    can it assert that form)

curving from the four corners, a cup, kylix
                    (a word, language),
below this the various branches

end in four-pronged stems,
          one, the longest, bearing the end-bud,
others minors, keeping proportion.
The whole thing somewhat isolated
          from the smothering multitude
a complete architecture of organic meaning.

Perfect to live, alone, lonely,
aspiring and self-fulfilled, growing, in a cleft,
                    on this high rock,
with only the wind and sky to see and hear.

7

But a flower torn off from the stem does not know
what a tragedy has occurred,
a waterlily

opens and closes with the day
on our table
as though it were a vase in a lake.

Rootless flowers!
whose individuation is yet a part of their form...

To live, become immune
to every bleeding cosmic wound.

8

The shapes, I think them
as of waves coming in
lapping the curve of the shore,
and wind carving clouds,
may be or not be as I perceive

but the fruit of the maple, pine cone,
seed of the cedar (proving Goethe's principle,
every compartment
a form like the flattened branch and whole tree)

formed out of the flux, are there
atomic, mobile—
unities that persist,
real as in a mind.

9

Who thinks the living universe?
I think it but in part.
Fragments exist
like those infinitesimal separate stars
I saw, lying on my back on the cushions
last night before the storm:

their union, as powers
but as wheels on the one axle,
and as form—

a drawing by a master hand.

We have united some few pigments
                    (all that is in museums)
but the greater part, all life, was there
                              united when we came—
and grows, a copious language of forms.

Who thinks them?...
            Their being is a thought.

My thought, a part of being—is a tree
of many thoughts, in which a yellow bird sits.

10

In the silence, sitting in the silence
I seem to hear the visible language speak

                                        a leaf

(a glimpse of paradise perhaps to be)

Here in hell, in purgatorio,
all things suffer this waiting, become
only then whatever they will be:
ecstasies of creation, flowers
            opening ecstatic lucent leaves.

Nothing else matters.
Nothing else speaks.

11

So beauty
it says, so quietly in the shadows
that a small bird
            on a red bomb
shrieks a symphonic whistle
just turning its head, without a sound from the throat.

Anywhere the eyebeam transects the world, a thorn
strikes with such sharpness to a thought.

LAC EN CŒUR

I had so far made it my concern
                    not to be aware
of writing a poem, thought of it
as irrelevant,
as in this case anyhow contrary
                    to in my real concern,

that I wrote nothing
                    I did not first think
complete, as it stands.
Not a poem, but a meditation—
          they make themselves, are also natural forms,

kernels that come whole to the hand.

LES RÉPÉTITIONS

I

Again Violetta's dying.
One would have thought once was enough.

When art becomes that real
      who wants it to be repeated?

And yet we do.
(its nice to have that first kiss again.)
In fact, nothing is much worth repeating—
      even the sex we vary
            as we do.

"Let's go to the movies."
      "Another cookie?"

The mystical experience is another thing.
Like art, it's something that should have happened
and therefore we repeat it.

(We are never bored
      with something that should have happened.)
"Let's do it again, maybe this time
      it will happen."

We repeat everything, looking for art.

II

*What you give some men never get
    not in a lifetime of looking—
        the difference
between sex and no sex
    is that between your speaking body
and any other woman.*

'Did you find art?' she said...

*If anything was that perfect
    we'd repeat it because it was perfect
just as we repeat what isn't
    because it isn't.*

FROM THE CHINESE

As the breeze rose (I guess there was a breeze)
the maple dropped its catkins with a rustle:
       I saw an explosion of pollen in the air.

In the morning light the leaves shone
       light green, like a lamp in the back yard.

FRAGMENTS 1

Ah yes, ah yes—the pieces!
Your broken pipe, John . . and the remnants of a dinner.
Only God is whole (like a work of art),
       and the greatest metaphor—
man enlarged to take in heaven,
       complete and perfect.
We are fragments torn off from creation,
and our poems fragments.
Therefore we find only pieces, and leave only pieces.

FRAGMENTS 2

We fools made our poems
           as fast as feathers of snow
and the winds took the torn flowers...

Nothing remains

The dry plains remember summer
and golden sunsets
           over back yards

Cats, clatter, and the tin horns
                  of yesterday

The children's hour that is no more,
           like the wind, like the snow.

THE DEMOLITIONS
(FOR JOHN GLASSCO)

I

The biggest name in Montreal these days is Teperman.
It stands a yard high, in front of old buildings:

TEPERMAN

Demolition

Teperman is working hard. I've seen the remains
of old dilapidated lovely city sections
                        go down in rubble—
"No Parking" signs over the lot.
And the whole city, including Cathedrals,
skyscrapers, the statue of Burns,
                        and our three universities,
level like these lots, as they will be...

Teperman works fast. What does he care
whether any building we want to stand
                        for eternity goes?

His business is DEMOLITION
                        and swinging metal balls.

II

The block on Stanley (I've got to check with the street
        post)
where our bohemia was just commencing
                        and the beatnik gallery burned
where Leonard had his rooms (offered in friendship
                        to MM GD and others)
where the Riviera coffee house and the tenements and
        Betty's "Tailor"

                              had their domicile
where Sutherland set up the First Statement
and we read the poem by Souster, in manuscript,
                              "The Groundhog"
and Madame No-wee-jee-ess-ka carried on....

So picturesque
          so picaresque
                    so European

Like the ruins of Warsaw, our only Latin Quarter
                    has been razed to the ground

I look at the empty space, and think of all the Hungarians
                    locked out in the world...

III

The new buildings that rise on the rubble
                    in flocks, to the langorous clouds,
will stand all night in their stories of light
                    swinging a searchlight to fear

but will not remember the slums
                    at the roots of their bones
nor the dead who went down on a Stryker frame
nor the unfledged young
                    who disappear.

Lonely for new glory they wait
          for long leaseholds and the penthouse dwellers,
their corridors filled with maidens
          too simple to love, and too ignorant to care.

A CIRCLE TOUR
OF THE ROCKIES

Even the chance relations
    of mountains to one antoher
blue against blue, are a kind of form.
I only make it by being where I am.

The jagged ones, also, a play of irrational forces
    as, at rock bottom, they say it all is—
but only to emerge, like an island, green out of chaos.

The purpose of disorder
    is to clear the slate for something new.

Think of mountains as an obstruction,
               Les Rocheuses of the mind.
It is all crowded there
    beautifully;
but beauty is a glut on the world.

Geophysically speaking, a magma
(orchids are likely to get crushed,
       many a tender thing).

And you get some of those sky-rocketing constructions
    or boulder-strewn barrows
        and thin glacial streams.

Clear it to the peneplane of un-being,
      an empty consciousness, space-time, a blank page,
and something begins again. God knows
maybe just a new area of suffering. Of experience.

For whom?
    This, for us, it happens to be.

A mountain of balsam, fir, spruce, avalanching moraine and
                                       [clay
    (mountains are top-heavy, always falling down),
like the universe, wearing itself away.

The frightful devastation of a forest fire
          seen eight years later,
like a cemetery, a battlefield, a Belsen of unflileted bones,
               may serve for an example.
(One doesn't like to see whole universes going up in
                         [combustion.
                    Put out that match!)
But it happens; in fact constantly.

There's a whole mountain like a flat empty wall
          waiting for decoration.
Your mind—could become that wall.

Or sometimes you get a stand of skinny trees
          that simply gotta go.
It's the heights and depths, in the hollow of vastness,
          for which it all exists.

Some of this, you don't know whether people have built it up
          or the forces of nature,
architectural theatres, stairs of erosion, strata.

The canyon of Nature
yawns to an infinite nowhere multiplying on destruction.

To cup an Okanagan
     folded somewhere in the belly of deformation.
It must be so desired! At least when had,
a superhuman satisfaction—
          to us! who are merely human!

(Don't forget we invented that thing;
but to think of it is to prove its existence—
you can't merely 'conceive' that your life exists.)

The first mode is non-existence,
out of which, by some twist of necessity, a world
          of superabundance comes.
Once they start it they can't stop
     piling mountains on one another,
rearing and eroding, until there's this—
an unpredictable satisfaction, like a girl to love.
It could have been some other, but it was something

you always had in mind.

It looks like a stone-quarry in some of these parts,
        as in strict definition it is.
The utility of nature, for man, is unquestionable;
but as in art, we are always asking: 'Is it a good in itself?'
It is. Anything that is good for anything
        is 'a good in itself'.

It has reality, for which, in the end,
        everything must have come to be.

Some of these things must be believed to be seen.
Though for that matter, we all see enough.
The thing is to work back.

Some people, you can give them the Rocky Mountains
and they want something. Unsatisfied.

Evenings, the deckle-edged hills help us:
certainly as something good, that speaks for itself.

And in the morning
the wave-movement of the hills
        like that wave-theory of matter
where fruit-trees flower in their folds
as the right wave-lengths gather in the Good.

I have believed that the whole universe is speech,
                        a communication.
That speaks for itself. And wants to be believed
                        to be seen.

Very useful, too, for us, who like to have something
                        to stand on

The mesocosmos
        in which we spend our lives.
Mack, Mike, Mess—the three worlds.
At least one thing in the Bible is true,
man is the first gardener.
Last night I read Genesis to Gregory,
                'a bedtime story'—
He created this He created that
                        (he didn't ask who).

'Enough?'
'No, read me more of that one.'
Like the red book about Zeus, Neptune, and Venus:
the twice-told tale.

G—(Geological process) created all the mountains,
the meaningful generations of matter.
Mountain begat stream begat field begat orchard.
The Bible of science.
(Bah, of course, equally absurd.)
But useful, to the Bomb makers and to children
                    at bedtime,
therefore real.

God is a brand-name for things
that come out of the chance factory—
            French beans, 'Made by God'.
            Christ—God, Inc.

Look. A sweet cunt of meanders
                    meeting on the hill.
Nature is playful.

And people come to the mountains
                    for mere pleasure.
Turn it into a cheap resort.
            The world
as entertainment, is no good in itself.

All kinds of amusement
and in the end we go into the Fraser Canyon
            (just before dark).
            What an experience!
And that is why God etc...

The Crucifixion according to one theory.
Eternal return, another.

Everything; there are even flatlands in the Rockies, swamp
soil and crushed ice in purling streams.

Real pleasure is a very gentle
                    occasional thing.
You don't go after it. Let it come.

And it's good sometimes to get that feeling
of the world looming over you suspended in space—
precipice, cliffs, and precarious ascents
            before the mind can come to rest.

Let it extend, as it does.
            It's something that just goes on.
Somewhere, everything happens.

We live in the most-possible-of-the-best of worlds.

Also of the worst, per contra.
            That's the chance one takes.

But the worst is a desolation
            somewhere outside our ken.
What we can bear to suffer,
            or enjoy, is limited
by what can do some good,
that has already emerged, as a kind of valley, or garden
            out of the void.

Clearly, the rest is up to us
            —whether there is 'meaning' or no 'meaning'
(the atheist and Methodist agree).
There are tones in that infinite landscape
intuitive of things to be.

But mostly the parched mountains, and poverty.
Ranch life, poor soil, sadness peering out of sunburnt eyes.
The skinny unhappy child and the mother
            in a cotton Sunday dress.

A poor universe, even if the best
                        possible.

Hot, dry, hemmed in by the mountains
that no one can traverse really,
slag heaps of unscalable rubble,
a cosmological waste
            leading nowhere.
You live here, trapped by their sloping sides
            and steep rushing streams,
a provincial in the great world—
            small, stunted, alone.

Are we concerned with small pleasures
        because the great are closed?
Prevented by mountains from seeing the scale of
        mountains,
            we stay on a stable-land or a plain.

The church itself is a hulk
            hiding the light of day,
and received knowledge, our science,
                    a glittering wall.

But the mountains are beyond conception,
        like the whole cosmos, that naturally is
unknown, inscrutable, incredible—

that we're stuck with—
        the immense sum of nothingness,
and the ecstasy of it all!
As if to say: 'Yes, at last! It is this I wanted!'
        'Yes, we are here—to see!'

But then, in the end, we sleep
            (withdrawn from circulation)
and the world goes on, building and dismembering its
                                [mountains:
the great small enterprise where we have a ticket
            for only one ride—
The Circle Tour.

Sad, when the merry-go-round stops.

Thank you.
It was exhausting, but impressive.
We lost our topcoats, of flesh and animal skin.

If there is anything we can remember
        It was the silence
in the great canyon of extinction,
and the loud invisible accord of things that live.

Violet last shadows of evening
                on the high cliffs.
Darkness is in the current, reflective colours.
In the mountains, even the dusk is brief,
            for sunset, over the peaks, comes early.

And the strenuous life takes its toll.

Then the cooler trees, cedar and fir, in the hollows,
damp, dark,
        thoughtful.

Turn away from it all.
What is it?

A circular movement of matter,
                swirling, atomic salt.
Distant, the dark trees, the snow patches,
        turbulence of waters
indistinct in the night—
a glimmer, a dot, lost
        somewhere in the void

where everything good is possible.

from

SELECTED POEMS
(*1975*)

ALBA

O Aphrodite
look down on the clover face of youth
                torn with desire
look at the lonely middle-aged
                   without satisfaction
look at the old in their flannels
                denied and played out...

Give every man a gentle responsive lover
        —and if more, a child of his own.

BRIGHTNESS

It is like love, this vision
taking us away from nonsense
              into a great silence.

Youth is over
          joystick, bicycle, the prowess of the body:
I would have it again, but more
           I would have it all erased
for some radiant future—

something it all contains and that contains it
like apples in autumn we have not eaten.

from

CROSS-SECTION:
POEMS 1940-1980

(*1980*)

THE DIVER

When your body dives into the lake,
                    among the bubbles, some
cling longer to the drum of your skin
than the rest, and when you lie in the sun
                              tight spheres of water
hang on to your brown shoulder, before the air takes them
away in vapour—then you run
                    and the air chases you
not wanting to leave you, and grass
                         catches gladly at your feet
How is it possible then
          that once you are near mc and pass me
my thoughts should not follow you
              also, like a train of servants?

IT WON'T COME SUDDENLY

It won't come suddenly
and there's no sudden end
  but in shiny shoes will you walk to it
   and with a nickel in your hand,
wearing that white dress of yours
or neat black suit
   (according to sex)
and white gloves to go with
     —just an ice-cream cone!
      — that's all it is!
what you've lived and lied for,
groped, ground your teeth and cried for
   A litte thing
But don't try yet,
the shoes won't fit
and the gloves will tear
even as you think of it
      And yet, my child,
    ice-cream can never be
     the same, without that trivial
     ritual.

A PACKET OF POEMS

Here I have been sitting reading French poems
that melt like mints in the mouth—
Apollinaire, Bernard, Cros—
who keep the breath coming quick and light
for hours, and the mind
like something tied up in ribbons.
It isn't that we have no tradition
nor that we have too much either,
but that we cannot offer, somehow,
new lamps that shine, for old.
See what fine translucent
lights these French poems make—lantern flowers!
Yet one could trace still their traceless
utterly transparent tendrils
that touch the ground somewhere,
feeding on rank breath and sudor.
But we, somehow, born blind on
a batteted planet, can find none
(or lack the talent to discover)
tendrils, roots, however fine, to transform the facts
of our systems into such poems.
So we die in leaf, not in flower.

HOW TO WORK AND RELAX
(FOR MADGE SIMPSON)

In the midst of the city's business depravity
the kids at least are doing something useful—
pouring sand into milk bottles
                    as they sit under the stairs
talking of their important affairs.

They work and relax better than factory hands
unable to think for the noise all morning—
who must play at pitch-and-toss
                        for a bit at lunch
to get the mechanical cricks out of their joints.

THE SPARROW

I thought of the insecurity of life, the difficulty...
when a small sparrow came down on the grass
                    almost at my feet,
his little black eye nervously examining me,
        and his head twitching this way and that.
I watched breathlessly his delicate soft movements,
        the light streaks of his back feathers,
the fluffy underside, and the diminutive beak—

'He has made beauty of his insecurity,' I said,
        'he has made beauty out of sudden death.'

MIDNIGHT MEETING

Whatever it is we'll die of it
I don't believe
      the Sphinx himself knew the answer
Still, a little here and there
        in this vast free expectancy
has point — violet eyes,
           cold fingers.

THE SECRET

Every poet at the beginning
has a lot to learn
      of what is all his own

a uniqueness gradually revealed

never too much, never exposed—
the secret hinted at, left to discover.

Methods as new mazes, leading all astray

until his circumventions and contemplations bring us
to that quiet stage

where he, the chalk-faced immortal
         stands mute and alone.

A TORN RECORD

Nothing that man makes, or believes, is permanent.
I have seen the ruins of cathedrals—
it is only a question of how long
        what is left of them can stand.
A thousand, two thousand years later, they lie forgotten.

Nothing matters forever, what matters now
is desire, at the center of the whirlwind
        where our two pleasures are folded in one rose.
What matters always is energy, how you can laugh,
        your mouth wide and wonderful against the wind.

BLACK BOY EATING
POP-CORN

See that little eatin' machine
        with skinny arm
                comin' down
        bendin' out
    putin' pop-corn in 'is mouth?

'That little old-style pop-corn pickin'
            contraption with knobby knees
    liftin' out from a long paper cone
             them white pop-corn seeds?

Yeah, that little black boy
        with eyes all 'live
            he seem to been born
    for nothin' but t' eat pop-corn!

LIFE & ART

She sings, sweet in all the streets,
    soft as a nocturnal love in arms,
with clashing colors, brazen breasts, hatless heads.
And if she won't, let her whistle off somewhere,
                let him be, first,
twisting onwards—life
            first, and art after, if a choice
                must be made.
Because she stinks, the old witch, when the demon
        fact has not loved her
up-in-air, a beautiful belly-of-a-girl.
And he is all goat without her by him ambling.

MORNING HOUR

Fried eggs & toast & coffee
at the Snack Bar
   an old poem to read,
      an essay
New Greek gurgles around
('George' is frying another order,
     the girl borrows his phone)
The essay rambles on...

I order more coffee, bite an oatmeal cookie
between bits of prose
    The poem is sweet and sad
     (Saint Guthlac happily dying)
And we are happily living
    today, O lovely today!
May it go on and on...

I put on my mitts and bever
    and walk out-of-doors

The vapour I breathe out is poetry
    the air I breathe in is prose.

A NOTE FOR
LEONARD COHEN

To borrow vine leaves
pay for books...
(awaken, world of memory)
By a field of timothy,
a stream for perch fishing,
with overhanging boughs...
There we sat, the cyclists of those days:
And now you smile, all literature,
our *yong Squyer*,
whose poems are as good as ours
ever were!
Are we to rejoice, in you,
warming our cooled marrow juices
by what you say?
Or, as you imagine, be young with you?
Or call age, a new
kind of power—
an authority over joy?
Nuts, to all that!
You may be free, of us, be perfect
pitiful, without a thought, as we
will look here and there
for such crumbs as still
half satisfy: but you are
ourselves, and suffer the same brief
no, no more—the whole story
takes in the lot of us.

AFTER HOURS

All this,
like the futile labours of the wind
            changing the shapes of clouds.

Something must have been made relatively stable
                in this world of flux
before man came, wanting eternity

Is that what all things desire?
        —to cease from change, create a permanence?
And man's invention, art, thought, and vision of heaven,
declare a secret in the will of things, partly realized?

FREEDOM

My two dogs
tied to a tree
by a ten-foot leash
kept howling and whining for an hour
till I let them off.

Now they are lying quietly on the grass
a few feet further from the tree
and they haven't moved at all since I let them go.

Freedom may be
only an idea
but it's a matter of principle
even to a dog.

THE POEM

To find a voice as natural
as my own words when I am talking
thinking or feeling—
                    just as it is,
a thought quietly flowing,
                    a silent language.

THE STRAY CATS

The stray cats whom my dear landlady persecutes
for whatever it is they do under her window
are so frowsy and bleary-eyed that I take pity on them
    and feed them sausages.

One of them has found a piece which I hid from the
                                            [landlady
under a car, and now he is tossing it
as if it were a mouse, giving it the random bite
    and rolling on his back in the dust.

These cats are not really hungry
despite the landlady's outbursts of raging hostility.
They do well from the cans—as I have heard at night
    jumping from my bed;
yet somehow I like to encourage that strain of rascality.

KINGSTON CONFERENCE

How green and cosy
        the campus looks,
          where the learned societies
meet, while atomic refuse is dumped into the seas
        (already killed several species)

And life goes on so stupidly
      outside — commonplace, uneducated, real
menaced by great know-how, or ignored
          by scholars,
while the beautiful trees, placid and uninformed,
        look on.

POETRY READING

I like to be at a meeting of poets
      where they read
Each proud of his art, stands up
and works his high effect

different from any other—
          strange, separate
as the grasses, or the species

Some declaim, others jest
some seem to suffer—for the sake of the game
      (as all do in fact)
some in the very clouds, some in dirt
but all devotional in their secular praise

of the actual and the endless ways
their syllables turn and return to contain themselves.

FAME

Fame! What a wonderful thing!
You can't sit down in a restaurant
    without having some stranger or acquaintance
come up with a hearty greeting.
Or palpitating girls, who've seen your name
      or face, on TV,
                stop you on the street....
(The public slobbers over your private affairs.)
Private life? You haven't got any!
                 Your barber knows
you're famous, and gives you ten extra minutes
      of conversation, between comb and clippers.
Your grocer puts extra items in your hamper
      out of good will—and charges for 'em!
Your milkman cheats you, for good measure,
                    to prove he cares.

Only your wife is indifferent,
treats you like a mat, or a pet dog:
      Here, eat this bone, stupid.

And the kids at home, they don't read.

THE FUNERAL

The only applause
at the actor's funeral
was the snow falling
more quietly than usual.

AUTUMN

All day the leaves have been falling.
I thought of snow,
but the ground is covered with yellow meal
            that you can put your foot through
as you go walking, in an eternal still.

Soft as air the dry leaves,
and the dried weed at my doorstep
            a thorny bone as beautiful
as the shape of anything when seen alone.

'It is all quite dead and finished,'
      you say, as you walk between houses and trees
holding your breath in mild wonder
            at seeing the ghost you will become.

TAO
(FOR F.R.S.)

Things that are blown or carried by a stream
seem to be living—not in that they oppose the wind
or oppose the water, but in that they move
                              lightly blown,
lightly flowing, like things that live.

We who are actually living do best when we do not resist,
    do not insist, when winds and waters blow,
but go gently with them, being of their kind,
in the secret of wind and water, the thought of flow.

SUCCESS

There's a moment at the top of the hill
when the old ills are over
and one sits gratefully in one's wicker chair
admittedly a bit complacent
looking back on the perilous falls
and the rock desert.
One sips one's julep (or it may be a light coffee)
as the afternoon closes and the long evening
opens its brown wings on a stage scene—
the moment in history
before the Scythians come
and the red blood is spilled on the white divan.

A SURPRISING CHANGE

Today, because I have loved you yesterday,
I am beautiful.
Observe my new angelic features.
The eyes' new light and sparkle, the mouth
red and glowing,
the vitality of flowing hair!
You have beautified my body with desire:
I see when I glance in passing at a mirror
the lights of it surround me.

from

CONTINUATION I
(1982)

So let's continue

These vast accumulations
          not without reason, that may have a use
or none

"Putting together lyrics'

With sex, talk, contact
                    between a sleep and a sleep—
a process you do not need to understand

And the stratifications of silence
as Wayson S Choy put it,
                    the mute affirmations of space

Beyond a few sentences, in our lives, there is nothing

But what did you expect—
          the poem to write itself?
or to start a hurricane?

Not really, only a language
to contain the essentials that matter, in all the flux of
                                        [illusion

Pebbles, that shine through the cobbled grey
                    that emerge, in time's liquid flow
as diaphanous heaven

And the viscosity of things
How it all hangs together
          hiding whatever it is it hides

The real world
is silent, we must be silent to hear it

Like the mind making poems
hid in the texture of language

An ecstasy after an ecstasy
to the quiet mind

I like to sit in the sky light
                coming from my window bathed in the light
Not strong enough hurt the eyes

As much vision as anyone can stand

The poetry of the commonplace
                (Dudek's "Snowbound")
goes on and on

The divine, if any,
                as Ducky-Lucky finds it

The absolute individuality of each living thing

Yet the problem, they say, is to decide
                whether man exists

("I don't want your fake poems
                I want a record of your mind")

Without a theory, as the light comes down

The delicately spaced syllables
out of their secret links and chains
                like strings of vapour

The trainwreck inside the heart
                in the meantime

Let the words lead us wherever they go
Each man's reality a psychodrama
                of excited crazy words

Then the quiet face in the coffin containing a life

O the poet that incredible madman
        possessed by what he hardly knows or comprehends
See him coming toward you, his fat checks on fire
convinced of his potency, his supreme art,
that no one needs or understands

One of God's handymen
for whom the future is still the word, hot out of chaos
and the present cracked mirrors, in which his own face
appears and reappears on every wall

He is possessed with possibility,
                        will create the world anew
until it burns out, or gives place to others
                                just as hot and new

Sometimes his models become become real and part of
                                        [nature—
                even for me and you

＿

Let the wars be fought by old men,
                conscript them in their sixties
("They have no aggression...")
                        "lumbago in the trenches")

Or generals, single-handed, with axes

Non-aggression, however, will not work against aggression
Slavery is not preferable

The more we try the more fanatic we make it
The best I can do now is to improve this verse

A spiritual diary

＿

Bleeding in the memory, like a wound in the mind
                that child with his hands raised
                                and a schoolbag around his arms

Evil, like roots, all over the place
O yes, you think that over the years you 'improved'
when everyone else can see you've gone to hell

In my opinion even 'French Canadians' are out of date
                                i.e. as a concept
There's no point in preservatives

Most of our ideas are out of date

                        Lemons on the lawn
                        The dandelions are blooming
                        Again in the spring

The Big Lie of the NEWS-papers
                        in 72-pt. Gothic,
the whole invented lousy mish-mash
                                of "the news"—
which has nothing to do with what really happens
                (as if that was so easy to describe)
but is only the putrid effluvium of venial minds,
a fiction for the conformists
                        in the miasmal "status quo"
(This will take you years)

And the indifference of the world to God, God
                (by God today we mean poetry)
which is reflection, upon death, reality....

I mean what the prophets always said,
turn your face against vanity, turn from your "false gods"

The media, spreading their shit music,
                        shit talk, shit advertising
flowing with simple lukewarm consistency
                        through the long hot afternoon
Voices of vanity, incurable vanity;

of triviality,
become the real, the commonplace, the everyday!

One gets to the point where one can't take it any longer
        Having attempted to clean the cloaca,
                you run from the stench at last
gasping far air

The fanatic ideologies competing for moronic multitudes,
        the organized religions disintegraring in their tombs

"A hell of a lot of inferior minds pontificating
        on the media," sd the panelist
Ideas get used up, like bubble gum, or toilet tissue
'Fucking" in the movies now compulsory
                (after *cinéma vérité*)
                        The idea of truth
reduced to what goes on in the lavatory...

And universities to be more concerned with "life"—
        i.e. with popular culture—studying the shit
                        under a microscope
POP goes the weasel. Magnified mink.
                New art in the corridors   All over the walls

The spread of illiteracy has reached the university

Poetry as forbidden music
                        La musica proibita
The black lynx of art

Mais le noir n'est pas si noir

The principle of indeterminacy
                in the mind, not in nature
(but so is all purpose or plan)

Thank God for necessity
otherwise we'd have nothing to depend on

Chance exists only in the mind, not in nature

Freedom therefore is certainly a possibility
        and is consistent with the necessary order
                of things

God, to put it differently,

necessity, God's will—
freedom, man's will and desire

God is the beauty of order sometimes visible

Man is part of that,
like flower, bird, or galaxy

In the fish, he swims
In the animal he leaps
In man he thinks

The fool insults God
The liar insults God with a lie
He insults himself, he insults God

Why mix that much together
unless you want something to happen?

"Where will a grain of sand be after the ice-age?"

The stone remembers?
desires...   hesitates...   decides?

Even estimates—approximates
And makes a mistake!

So the computer: "Now there is."

All it needs is a sex-life

*

To be born again, to be born new
        be whatever grows, whistles, groans
(The broken rhythm becomes a new rhythm)
Go with the current against the current
                Dance with the soft shoe

An egg, an embryo, a perfect world—
             a chaos unborn

Chaos, a cloud, a new beginning—
             a new order

An arm, an outlet, an empty appendage
        to hold the future

A mouth, a missile, an open tomb
         to a new world

In self-indulgent turmoil, where angry words slumber,
the serpent in glass, with eyeless fury,
              gathers his testament
on a timeless trail, to the heaven we spawned...

Metal, wood, flower, form,
the various particles of ethered air

All objects we knew, fractured, impure,
gathered in that museum of glass

Silence, the perfect center

Poetry is dream pouring over
                              into life

A clothesline of girls
              dangling skip-rope & satchel
drag along the curb—to swish & chatter—
              as a car swerves...

Leering at licence plate—angry collision of looks—
A jamboree of wheels— the ropes unravel—
              rear, reroute, ride

A teenage giggle of gears and bearings
                              follows like a rain
or a wind in the washing

What is life?   Preserved when warm
                              cold it decays
Death is a frigidaire

O men of the future
As you walk along your gleaming corridors
              anxious and adjusted
              active yet ill-at-ease

think of us
       and the human truth we wanted
              to shape the pure aesthetic line

Who want a permanence, though it may be
things seem fixed are only moments
                              in some great change

Ah, how we try to please you
        and how little we succeed!

The dazzling daylight, the girls' flimsy dresses—
        delightful green things

How it all shines, shimmers, and coheres
A kaleidoscope (Stevie boy,
                you would have loved it)
And say that it is good

A bird's eye-view
It shoots down Atwater like a salmon
to its river and its lake-like curves
                turning to spume at Ville LaSalle
Around it meanders from the city's long shoulders
        Baie d'Urfé & Ile Bizard
the Lakeshore shallows sleeping around Ste Anne

Then descends, a shot-silk around the body
        of the beautiful island, thickening at the thighs
Back River, Île aux Coudres, Île Jésus,
        Pointe aux Trembles, Bout de l'Île

Here in front of us below the rapids
                Au Pied du Courant—
opening the port to all the seas,
lovely and lyrical, like a long-legged Lilith
she raises her breasts and lifts you to love

The lonely mouse is talking to God,
        he says um-um

God likes what the mouse says
God shows him another piece of the world

Poetry invades the air—
        small guns exploding in tousled hair!

Volleying down corridors
          arms spread and screaming
the young have taken over
           with LSD

"We are the victims, in vertigo, in vortex
We have lost control, we have abandoned
              every article of conformity"

Let other poets thrive (as we grow older
          memories thin)
      —who want the final judgement in their time

We'll have each other
and wait for this, while violence and wars increase

As for glory
get the moment down on paper
          for an eternal slumber

And if anything remains, remember—
        there was love, also a remnant

from

ZEMBLA'S ROCKS
(*1986*)

THE INEFFABLE

Straight from the frigidaire, the black grapes,
newly washed, glisten on the table.

Like black words in a poem, they cluster together,
      each shining with its own light—

the real meaning hidden somewhere inside them.

MORNING LIGHT

The sun, bright lemon, from the blinds
falls on the dusty books and papers
In my room
            A thing of white skin and tissue, I
perform yoga on the floor.

                        Look at my body
drifting in the sun. It dissolves
flaccid as water plates in summer
in the little Niger river.

                  But the sun
is a changeless metal, the minted light of a star
inside my room.

HILARY OUR KITTEN

Hilary our kitten
appearing like a virtuous thought
        in the midst of depravity,

a divine efflorescence, live, out of mud molecules,
like golden constellations in the summer grass
        while a pall of cloud passes—

comes back shining, with twinkling star-eyes,
comes out of nowhere, as nature's coup-de-grâce
        to solid stone ice-face:

gentle Hilary, kitten-conscious
come to purr, among God's little tea-sounds,
            furrily welcome.

FOR YOU, YOU

For you, you, whoever, wherever you are
in time to come, in a year or in fifty—
who have grabbed me, found me on the cluttered bookstall
and gone, book clutched in your hand, or stuffed in pocket,
to the near café or steaming snack bar

and over the pie and coffee opened up the pages—
for you, quiet girl, young man,
in the youth of your life, who read some pieces
then turn to your own thoughts, your emotions
and write your own eight lines, or fifty—
yes! yes! I would arouse in you
           the spectral nerve
sweet as sex, for this craft—
its breath of life wafted out and recorded
that it may be such a stir one time, for you.

A WARM NIGHT

I walk in the warm wet night,
the streets glisten, the lights glimmer,
the air like chamois, night-soft with silence.
All things are possible,
The wind wraps a scarf around my middle—
o lift of sweet seduction.
There are dark corners,
lumps of black, diamonds of possibility,
and people storing their pain
in dark houses, with few windows, under the lit cross.

The city sleeps, while the night searches its hidden recesses,
                    with secret seed.
It leaves the city heavy with those deposits of daylight's
                                        [progeny—
            whatever we do or dream.

I walk in the echoing streets searching
the opposites that meet, or trap the constellations
and the beautiful dark, in my net, as I lean
            over the edge of night.

A NIGHT OF TROUBLE

Tortured with sweet distress, mooning over old letters,
I dreamed your soft face
                that vulnerable flower
in the wet cold, near my hand

And your body in a nightshift
like a mangled rose, unreachable...

You told me it was not enough
            (whatever it was, it was not enough),
wanting more, more...
                And I awoke.

FIRST LOVE

You wore a blue coat and white scarf, remember?
And we walked in the dim night-time, talking.

What does love matter, or all that since has happened?
What has happened is an eternal possession.

When I am dog-tired or have been sick and almost dying
I sometimes wake as from a living death, and then

it is suddenly as if I were with you again, walking arm in
        arm,
and I say. "This life and we both are deathless in that
                                              [trance."

What angel marks the moment that will be remembered?
And what knowledge, perfect in us, touches its high
                                        [clouds?

We have stored this love and that despair like seeds of
                                        [strength,
so that we can never say, of any joy, that we have lost it.

Come, kiss me in your quiet way, in this place of memory,
and let us not be sad that we are old now, and dull of love.

Your eyes water in my dreams, and I see your face pale as a
                                        [wafer
that I am bending over and kissing under every street lamp.

TREMOLO

In a pale sky

        one star

lonely teardrop

        for the ills of the world

(if anywhere in nature

        such grief gathers)

still

    trembling there.

REGRET, REGRET

'Oh, when I was young! when I was young!"
sang an old grey bird for a winter song.
"I could hear the grass rise on the head of a worm,
I could feel the sap beat in a twig in a storm,
        when I was young."

He flew at the wind that ruffled his crown,
This nostalgic bird with a trick in his tongue,
having sprinkled the air with mournful notes
that of old had burst from numberless throats:
        "When I was young."

But he broke no heart, allayed no pain.
What the bird died of was a gun, I guess—
or a seed stuck in his craw somewhere
that he'd never coughed up into the air
        when he was young.

THE EPIPHANIES

As the light fell on a piece of rayon,

                my wife's underthings

the moment of revelation

Or evenings, at sunset, at Pine & Park

                when the lights come on

you can get it any day

And there's a blue motel

           on the way to Ste Agathe

                somewhere.

MAEVE

I see your moist face now before me
          drawn in pain lying on a pillow
Does the world know how many ways
             you may appear?

Only I know your beauty
Only I know the many ways
          (even in darkness)

You are like a coin made of silver
        like a fragment of ancient metal
                My broken beauty

How you do take me, in many ways
How you do trace the shape of eternal desire.

THE YOUNG LOVER

Wherever he went he found again
some girl as soft and simple as rain,
or if lie did not find, he made her
out of spindly legs and a far gaze,
so that soon her parents stood amazed
at her touch, like truth, and straight look
and love in her eyes like an open book.

NON GRIDATE PIU

The dead have nobody to protect their interests—
                    the living publicize themselves.
The dead lie quietly on the shelves, neglected and
                                        [ignored—
          the living have the floor.

Think of the dead, unable to stir a limb
                    or to move to a microphone—
while the living broadcast to the world
                    their desire to be heard.

Think of the dead, silently still
                    in their folded pages—
while the living make all the noise they will
                    to drown out the ages.

ORIGINS

Bright daylight is our victory
a world of doves, white hares in the snow,
made friendly by the spirit of selection and affection
        like a sentimental landscape:
practical streets we can ride in, homes with doors,
women with two breasts. a mouth, delicious pudenda,
names of friends, numbers on phones, titles or deeds.
We made this order with stagecraft of art,
for pleasure, for peace, for use.

Beyond that, chaos, angst,
the smudge of faeces, a trail of blood
leading into the flaming furies—
beyond our nature, this world's enemy.
The mind totters before annihilation
                like a creator
on the brink of his created world!

What was it before we pushed back chaos?
A piece of chaos? a wind?
Enslaved by the hot stars in space, torn and sundered—
the dismembered gods that we are, assembled?

Or nothing? We were nothing
before we became. But not nothing
before we came. Something moved
that led to this form—to the hand, to the human eye.
Out of that other nature we became.

HOLY UNIVERSE

The delicate violet of the chicory,
dwarf daisies—real!
                  (the actual)
Revealed in the needles and the nebulae,
        as the incurved dandelion
reveals itself, as the tiger lily
                      its obscene self,
or the red-fluted moss I cannot name.
Manifest, emergent, what they are:
            the clover a threeness in its mute mind,
            seeding infinitude of threes,
the tulip tree the cup of its leaf—
                    millenia pressed in coal.
The fiddle of the vetch, its pinnate leaves
                deployed over the fields.
Holy universe
            whose forms I write as I write my form,
            revealed as the gods they speak of
                    and as secret.
I am not curious to know more than the eye can see.
The real is all the real that is real, made real.

CHRISTIANITY

Into the animal nature came the idea of love,
the animal was changed. The wolf-heart of man
chastened with a priority: something deep imbedded
that even the brown oil-eyed animals have—
the sad heart of love sleeping in feral nature.
Perhaps what all creation yearns for,
    the rough-gentle grasses razored by the wind,
    and the flying metal meteor, cruel as cutlass:
"Give me peace, give me rest, somewhere in heaven."

We die. Eat flesh, Suffer and give pain.
With glass tearless eyes have come through time,
                killer and killed.
The hand is stone, with blood of necessary sacrifice.
But into that hard waiting came unlooked-for relief,
a crack in the mouth of clay, a broken smile:
    the face still hurts, for most, whenever the dry mud
                                    [breaks.

VANISHED BEAUTY

'Art' is whatever endures, of the past,
and only what is made of durable stuff endures.

But who knows whether things that have happened
    —gestures, speech, an embrace—
were not more memorable, more worthy of art,
                and yet have perished?

Who knows, but the greatest moments have vanished
            without a record?
as our lives have vanished, our youth,
                vanished without leaving a trace?

ATLANTIS

It appears in fragments.
        or whole, at certain moments—
real in every detail,
itself, or a false shine
           of the real thing.

Else life would be a vast train wreck,
with all its items of foolish baggage,
        combs, nighties, make-up
           scattered over the tracks—

and nothing in it.

AN EPIPHANY

The most living, the most mobile,
           is eternal'd in art:
the invisible, visible only in the form
          of the perishable and mobile,
made immobile and imperishable
           fixed and formed
in the dead matter of ink and paper—
         that lived and wavered
trembling over the perfect word.

LETHE

Young, you discovered the world—
the taste of oranges, rupees of coffee,
and firewater sex.

Then, it was change, change—
the demolitions of a collapsing order,
                                    as slow decay of the body
and passion withdrawn to the ruins of time.

Now it is solid substance—
                a handshake, for feeling,
and a wan smile of recognition
as ghosts begin to know each other in the gathering gloom.

AS MAY FLOWERS
(FOR BERNHARD BEUTLER)

In this month, the bones unsticking from their death
for a short resurrection,
pale puff-balls of lilac and popping mock-orange
bend on the bush, and the weeping ash
lifts a languid arm to greet the spring—
the life we love but cannot have,
the eternal, the recurrent,
                its grape-gardens of ecstasy,
in which we only taste the new-made wine
once, before we go down to oblivion,
to feed the earth for a new season.

from

INFINITE WORLDS
(*1988*)

SNOW SEQUENCE

The hoar-frost on the branches
against the red brick of the house opposite.

Again the famous wave of Hokusai,
the water wrinkles of D'Arcy Thompson,
the stars in their galaxies—
but mainly it is the hoar-frost on the branches.

As Pound would say, "The frost is the frost."

2

"A leaf is a leaf"
             but he did not consider
that this is already the way
of 99 per cent of mankind.

"She told me she bought a new dress."
"And I ran into Joe...

Who never rise to a new generality
out of the blinding bog of particulars.

3

The blue night of the soul
opens its little fingers of light
into my dark recesses.

It explodes in sparkles of tiny hope
and delicate flowers of sympathy.

4

What bores us in poetry is its untruthfulness.

Let poems be true, even if trivial,
like our dreary lives.

5

Greatness exists
because man suffers from insignificance.

He invents great men
and grants this tribute grudgingly, to only a few,
in order to keep up the illusion
that not all is insignificant, that greatness exists.

All worldly status, honor, rank and promotion,
compensate for nonentity, create a fiction of human glory.

6

The masters of the recent past, our fathers,
should at least have taught us self-honesty.

Hesse, Gide, Ezra Pound—
                          each of these
had paid everything for a little truth.

7

The snow's innumerable tiny swirls
                          can never create a universe.
There, the logic of infinite combinations
must fail. Only the same old new-old forms
repeated ad infinitum—
            like the sea you once celebrated
as "ever unchanging"—
                          nothing but snow
making its different shapes, 'The Forms of Water.'

An infinite end in itself,
            incapable of a new creation.

8

But now it is melting on the branches!
            Colliding atoms,
                shrapnel of snow!

— 201 —

And in the high trees
whorls in the circular heavens
                    of cherubim and seraphim.
the hierarchies of angels.

Those 'tiny tears'
            have made a paradise
for dutiful mankind.

Even the snow is more than the snow.

MOON°

Sitting in the branches
of trees at midnight.
I drink moonlight.

When the sky is brilliant
I sit in the branches
and drink deep.

Moonlight is too strong for me:
I mingle it with the waters
of separate stars,

I mingle it with the stars
in the bowl of night,
and drink deep.

---

*   The next five poems are from an earlier time.

A WHITE PAPER

Butterfly wing,
silver diver of the air
held in my pocket,
who danced of your own free will
with the dancing wind,
was lost in a cloud
and then came down
to a lawn,
to a rooftop,
missing the rooftop,
to a street, to the edge of the sidewalk—

you, destined to return
to rest in my hand,
belong in a book to keep for a keepsake!
Shall I place you in a museum?
You are a record of me, as I of you.

Once, I traced with my finger
the delicate ribs
and bones of a dancer
who died in the sea
and buried his body in stone;
Dalmanites... today's museum piece, I saw
playing among corals
in a green sea,
dancing among sunbeams,
running from a shadow.

So you be a record of me,
a print I traced with my eye
one afternoon
that someone time hence
may lift like a layer, and see
me, white in the sunlight.

A STORE-HOUSE

There is a small store-house of knowledge in which
    I sit sometimes on hard wooden cases
leaning against stacks of material kept there for use;
the door is ajar, and I can see a lawn,
some buildings, a segment of street
where people pass. But no one looks in through my door.

I sit, leaning and looking at the samplings I get
of the world; I meditate about it:
of the numbers of girls in colleges compared with men,
    and of the future of society;
of the muscles of coloured coal-heavers opening a man-
    hole;
of labour, power, and ignorance;
of the idiocy of avarice, of fear, and of the danger of ideals;

of the pity of people, that plod like dray-horses or
    senseless nuns
set on a narrow plank of purpose, with their beautiful
    wandering eyes
shielded by habit, the death and anodyne of life.

And sometimes I want to cry, and sometimes to call out,
to raise a banner before my shack, make up a congregation.
But I know that no one will look into my door—
the people pass by too busy.
    God knows, I will go out
and walk in the streets.
Perhaps I will meet other men sitting in doorways, sad
    as I am;
if I find them, we will sit aside somewhere
and talk this over.

O CONTEMPORARIES

In a cloud of time, this dust of locusts, in which we move
Involved with Stalins, Churchills, and chorus girls' legs,
Who is the Gulliver to shake the earth with a feather,
Unravel the tongues of the winds and make them talk?

They say any man—a locust—in every crook of his wings
Can in an empty treble, yet enough to fill a space
With the sharp, sure, useful whistle of the flywheel,
Make our intelligence like the intense cricket sing;

But it fails, and frays like wire in dissonant noises,
Hurts the heart awhile, dies away, and leaves no sound;
There is no noise of knowledge left, but only the clatter
Of caricatures, a Hitler circus, jitterbugging kids.

Gather together the broken teeth of light scattered
From Rockefeller's skyscrapers, and the bones of numb
    neon.
Re-assemble them. What records of reptiles' jaws,
What beasts are these? Take them to the museum,
    and ask.

Let the white-frocked boys tell you of time's serpent,
Of man in his naked skin, who is vulture and fish
And cell in a slide, like a swollen eye trailing
Out of the womb he came from like a blazing star:

But not what dimensions of space he sleeps in, what times
He sweeps as he multiplies, what gods he gives joy to;
Nor what is this storm-blind moment that we tread,
What this unsteady stone in space on which we cross.

AS MIND,
THE TOY OF REASON

As mind, the toy of reason,
complicates the infirmities of middle age,
so the figurative chaos of multiplicity
is charged with patterns, of things,
utilities, money values—
those irrelevant inventions
to a properly feeding organism,
shovels to feed, crates to take the air in.
But beyond the prisms of mind, where the greedy
            intellect never reaches,
colors gleam and flare, coruscate like the great aurora,
with a passion of life, a passion of pure existence.

from

CONTINUATION II
(*1990*)

The beastly cold, and the heaven of your arms
Between the two, we make compromises

Taking attendance, God is 'absent'
Or always 'present', if you like

Invisible, unknown, it comes to the same

The undetermined numerator
                          in a very small fraction

Then Man in the mass   group thinking
               —infantile, ferile, insane

with concentration camps
          (a sick inmate supported by friends
to save him from being shot
                    for not standing)

And the bodies in Belsen forest
                          the refugees' faces
or death carts, in Warsaw

Be patient, as a plant on the window-sill is patient
'Turn me, turn me'

That wall, will be there tomorrow
Which kind of contradicts your notion
                         that everything's in flux

"Its all violence, chaos, unrest," said Sirhan Sirhan
"Whatever happened to the old days, peace and quiet?"
                                    (he wanted to know)

As for the bureaucrats, Spender says
                    "They are not willing to wither away"
They never will

"After fifty, those who are qualified
                    devote themselves to philosophy..."
                                            (Plato)

Lord, let me have wings
            in my late years, when baldness comes
Open my skull to heaven like a mirror

Let me think nothing but
        eternal thoughts, out of that dust and gravel,
the ashes of existence

Make new hope possible, for future birds
            Laugh at wounds, tear all obstacles aside
and show, naked, the creative chromosomes.

—

The great white flags, like bladders, in the distance,
the cooing and crackling of birds
                    (doing their own bickering),
under the soft sponge of heaven,
                    of time, that erases

So what's happened to poetry?
            Even the poets have lost interest (the good ones)
The rains came, a drizzle
            of words from all quarters

Today my face seemed small
            when I put my hand to it
Have I become less?

A rain-washed grey over the world

What is it, about the sky after rain,
      the light green, the clouds like white cream,
and tree branches embroidered with buds?

Uncommon greyness silvers everything

                    ～

Like a bevy of birds the children came running
            on the way to school
                  —morning's little floral decorations

After the rain,
the first words, something that, re-worded,
            leaves nothing to be desired

Falling on stone, or air into water
                              As now

I sit here listening to the leaves grow.

                    ～

This morning, at dawn,
I walked out and saw the quarter moon
in a pale-lit sky and the looming trees
over the quiet street, where a single bird fluted
his morning song. I stood among the flowers
    listening on my backyard lawn.

All day I carry within me
        the silence of the dawn...

The judge is up there, who pronounces lastly
We live only for that heaven
        which does not exist

"Art" is the meaning of history,
        something that "must be preserved,"
that must endure, at least for a time

—that evaporates slowly
        like tea, cloves, laurel or lilac

We preserve it in jars,
        we preserve kitchen recipes

Say it was in freedom we made it
The winds carried us to where we are

God's kickapoo juice, with all the ecstasies, intensities

Soaked in the emotion of autumn
                    a wind like a lost dog
squalls through the backyard
                    shaking the garbage cover...

Black minatory branches
stare through yellow trees

The garden has collapsed
like a fallen clothesline on tenting sticks,
                    even the flags of weed
turn away from the disgrace of summer
like beggars from an abandoned feast

⎯

First the fiction, then the meaning of the fiction

Cf. the characters of James' late novels
                    ('the master of them all'),
telepathic people who talk inexhaustibly
                    (sometimes saying finally what it is they mean)

All that is not indirection is 'vulgar'
Hence a cloud-screen of words becomes
                    a verbacious figleaf

It satisfies beautifully
            but may not precisely enlighten us:
"You don't, you know, really tell us anything,
                                    Master."
And don't you think it was vulgar,
                    really, rather vulgar,
to be so terribly concerned with all that heavy money,

never to be able to rise, to be able quite positively to rise.
        above mere class value with its conventional arse-hole
                so well settled in property—

never to be able to see a real 'idea,' a real bit of sex,
            or a real lump of art, as we know it...

"And what, pray, are these?"

Books, books, books

We'll all be buried under the ruins

In roiling and boiling methane
the city bus lets go a great blue fart
                    into a crowd of schoolchildren.

Education under gas (USA)
A fish in a goldfish bowl was trying to explain the universe
but didn't even get as far as the Second Law

Nor did I.
A manifestation of talent?
My teachers never saw anything special
                    —perhaps they were right

One said I had the gift
        (McBain on "The Literature of Power")
We were all geniuses then

Who is the great one? By god, no one,
                            if you look close
But those who ask for nothing, may find it

Poetry is not a solitary vice,
it involves the whole damn world
                    and that's why failure hurts

Not for success, who needs it,
        but "Not another failure"
                        as Chaplin said

Listening to music mostly,
                like passing small stands
of trees in a train, a soft blur

(Better to play one adagio
than do the whole sonatas and partitas
                            in one afternoon)
Wachet auf!
Wrote it to sing in church—
                no 'great man' after all
(Failed to get the job, despite six Brandenburg Concerti)

        Or Frank Scott

blind in one eye like Yeats
who saw with rational clarity
the monopolists, financiers, speculators
puddle our national wealth
                into one private pile

The facts,
the significance of the detail,
                as I saw on a packing case
HECHO EN MEXICO.

The secret key to poetry
B-natural
C-sharp etc.
        (whether minor or major)

And never hit a flat.

After the poetry reading,
sitting in Union Station
                thinking that I had mentioned Chaplin
in two of the poems... and was there a third?...
when the Muzak in the station
                began playing "Limelight."

A word from on high.

Maybe, maybe
            And maybe not

Those unique events
            are always happening
They are in the nature of things
                                Chance
the surprise factor

God, precisely, plays dice with the universe
That's how it happens (at least
                it's one of the elements)

Bombs falling on Berlin,
          London, 1943

Gottfried Benn
stationed in Poland
               wrote
"These eighteen months were the quietest and
          happiest of my life."

How far is Gorzow from Lidice, from Katowice?

And there was a conference of theologians
                         in Wroclaw,

where they came up with "kerygma"

(Influence on Norrie Frye).

Man, in general, is "badly adapted" to life in this world

Cleaning the cat-shit
          Everything you love
carries some obligations—the universe
                    does not run itself

The environment
is not fit for humans, you have to ignore
                    most of it

Poetry is another thing

In the midst of murder and mild hysteria,
          you live and write

Put a penny in the word-box
               and hit the jackpot

It's the verbal fall-out
               that matters

And yet sometimes, we're walking on air,
          in a kind of spirituality
of pure being

The words are floating,
gathering the ether under the t's,
               flown by the vowel jets

In this world yet not of this world.
In the eternal element we are

The state is still the grand protection racket,
                90 per cent of all taxes extortion and tribute
paid to keep the bureaucracy in lard

Yet there's one thing worse than empire or nation,
a revolution, the grand chaos
that follows the collapse of that efficient
                                exploiting machine

Literature, art
an unnecessary superstructure

An adjunct to religion,
of a feebler, personal, more complaisant kind

Unusually ignorant as dirt
           of the dirt on which it feeds

Primed to self-destruct, if the truth seeps in

Madness as mythopoeia, poetry as mere opinion,
                or the desperation of the ill-attuned
to blood, murder, genocide and war

And of course we're usually well-heeled
           when the message is right for the times

i.e., aesthetically in the swim,
           if the future "time of troubles"
has been our theme

And it's the final seal of our purity
           observing the butchers of mankind,
to hold up the standard, for no other purpose
           than to be well-approved—
to hold up the Tables of the Law
           before the worshippers of pork!

Ah, when perfection was "other worldly"
           the real somehow contained more of the good
than it does now, when we want to find it
           entirely in the actual and diurnal.

Until the sixties,
    literature in the high sense,
        at least in the mind of a few, survived
but since then, even in anthologies,
          even in the schools, it has vanished

A few individuals, unknown, unrecognized,
    will be lighting the first candles
           in a dark age

Like that time, in tears, I stood listening to Mozart,
and saw him a companion to my griefs

With everlasting joy I raised my arms
        to the eternal and immortal
above all pain, to which great art belongs

We live among the ruins
      of mere appearance,
in a slush of habit

We 'break up' with laughter, and go to pieces
    at one gargantuan joke at the end

Death's the epitome of laughter,
        the grand dissolution
for which small dissolutions prepare

Nature, a nihilist, likes a new beginning
    at every turn

Poetry is like religion, lunatics and crackpots
                latch onto it

But when you hit the earth you know it,
           so when poetry gets too prosaic
it comes down to trivia,
              the facts without significance

A modern Inferno, minus the terza rima
            how to get out of it

                          ➤

There are delusions, even as in religion

Well, as Conrad said "Ah
           if only I could write ze English good—
                       I mean, well!"

"Do not be conformed to the world
                    but renew your mind"—
i.e., renew your internal environment
                        (St. Paul)

Like the sky, that clean inscrutable blue
        that remains always new

So, at last you knew, Ezra
That the present stands forth,
              stands forth, once death beckons
Outshines yr Verrochio, Varchi & Broglio

That people precede art, precede judgment

And then the present shines like a dishpan,
shines like small faces, of those ragazzi,
           the little people

Shines like wild mustard, a precious metal

As you in your silence knew, in your eyes the tears
            the while Dadone spoke
                    the love letters.

To make the world levitate
                in a kind of ether,
to make the real miraculous

The beginning is everywhere
                The end is everywhere

The child of two, told to 'throw a ball'
                brings it to your hand

The thought comes to you on the page

One of the mysteries of the creation
        in which we are embedded

The perpetual coitus interruptus of poetry

Death's jab in the loins:
"What did you have in mind?" she said

Nothing

"Human tears are a re-creation of the primordial ocean
        which bathed the first eyes"

But the heart knows heaven is somewhere
                far away

The eye "a piece of the brain which has budded"

And what the eye sees the brain records

A blind acceptance of the given
                flowing happily along

In Hardy's day
  "strings, clarinets and serpents"
        it used to be

& the reading of classics from Milton to Pope

(Our popular bks
   like a whirlpool in a toilet bowl)

Portland & Purbeck, stone for cathedrals
        then
for distant churches
"from Rampisham to Bettiscombe"

And your greatest genius
   was "a pale, gentle, frightened little man,"

In the backyard of the mind
a flower blooms

We create gardens out of the mere scent of roses

Their falling is like flowers,
     gardens of syllables

shaped by invisible hands, or led gently
   by the intelligence

where everything good comes to flower
   in pattern and design,

making the grand Choral Symphony
   of the world.

       ━

I would want it perfect
  and natural as the speech of children,
tumbling deliciously
    into the prurient present

Like the blossoms of the maple, against the grey sky
   a yellow green mealy scatter

No ghost fighting like wind in a tarpaulin

but a quiet ether-cooled dreamer

a floating lilypad on the smooth skin of time

And all the long afternoon,
              not even memories seduce me
A strange detachment, as if things did not matter

Shadows of leaves, a curl of cypress
            Listen, we all are helpless, before the slow pull
of time, yield to it gently
                    See how quiet

the empty air and the infinite sky
beckon and welcome "all who enter here"

I walk as gay as Christmas into the morning sun,
     tremendous delirium in my bones

To this little eternity, returned

The chromosomes, my cornerstones
God is no puritan

"The holy life of music and of verse," sd Wordsworth

Art is kinesis, a true spontaneous rhythm,
while actual living is like stone
                    too hard to cut
or unpredictable splitting crystal
                        recalcitrant to form

Therefore we permit art, the true language of being,
              subject to no compulsion—

its internal dynamics the only true definition

Intellect lights up the world,
but God doesn't have his mind made up

Hear the birds going like lemon squeezers,
            in trees of candy-floss—
to the dim rhythm of remembered dreams.

Yes, we are like God's birds
                    in our cage of a world,
know where the feed-box is, and the water,
            the little swing,
and the wires of the cage we can hop to—

but what's beyond we can't imagine,
        can't conceive, the real, the great thing,
as a bird can't conceive the quantum theory

Don't notice that miracle

Straight from the clouds
                    by chance
out of nothing, everything comes of nothing,

the unrelated particulars that make up a world

Even as a single mind cannot be classified
                as to what it thinks

Creativity neither random nor rational,
        a surprising new mixture,
                    with a flair for design

Pink peonies, candy floss
                of gigantic size

Or luscious lettuce leaves
used to support chunks of lobster, avocado,
                and left uneaten

A unique event that happens
                        as it happens

The poet in old age
        between Orpheus and Morpheus,
cut off from the media,

thinks that Jaws
            is a movie about dentists.

Remembers sex
as something he missed
                    in youth.

Finds the serenity of old age
an illusion.

Spends his days meditating
            on things he will never do.

(Might take up a second career,
if he knew what he always knew
                    he wanted to do.)

Sleeps well, the first part of the night,
            and any part of the day

When asked, says he's o.k.
Doubts that you would listen
            to the whole story, anyway.

—

I believe in the plainsong,
        "rendre à la poésie...
                de la vérité, du naturel,
                        de la familiarité même"

As he said, "S'accoutumer à écrire
        comme on parle et comme on pense"

We had a conversation, asking
                        what a poet most needs—
starting from Pound's answer
                                "curiosity"

And one said "receptivity"
                another "endurance"
                        and a third "to loosen words"

I said, "A sense of beauty, feeling for beauty"

Claritas, radiance,
        or "the blaze of being,"
whatever in a leaf, a line, or my cat sitting,

something that shines
                "of a mystery"
                        i.e., the radiance

For the poet has "a nature exiled
                        in the imperfect
which would possess immediately, on this very earth,
                a paradise revealed."

Think how, in the cold of outer space,
                              among the burning galaxies
this garden world
              has come to be

For a brief duration
                  of becoming,
the flowers pure colours, the birds
        singing their crunchy notes

and little old ladies, with children in the park

Whether through gods (God) or mere happenstance,
                  here we are

amid the cold of space, the fires of outer heaven

There may be infinite worlds
Why should all there is
              be contained in what we see?

Diogenes of Cappadocia wrote on the wall
        his brief comfort to the world

"There is nothing to fear from God
              Death is harmless
          Some good is possible
        Most evil can be endured"

And we have Homer's little enjambments
                          and lyrical book-ends

        keládont epi oínopa pónton
                              Zephirus
singing over the wine-dark sea

But when it's over, we know, don't we
      this life has been magical

that we were lifted once
             out of ourselves
writing these poems

and looking at people
             in distant places—

the magic of the voyage
             to other worlds

And then the sea, the sea
             remember

and the clear rolling breakers out there
             dying out in the sand

by the white washed sea-shell
             lying on the shore.

—

from

SMALL PERFECT
THINGS

(1991)

THE ULTIMATE

All that we have left
        of some ancient poets
is what happened to be quoted by this critic or that
        in a rhetoric book.

Bits and pieces.

This is the ultimate distillation
of a life's work—what the world knows.

And you have no control of it.
It's paltry, a beggar's mite.

Even now
the only part that most readers know of you
is what they find quoted by some critic or other
        to illustrate a flaw.

WHAT WE PROFESS

In Greece it was a merchant
        who started a school of philosophy,
and a stonemason who taught Plato
        how to seek truth.

We who specialize in the discipline
        no longer know what we believe—

since those who teach know less than those who do.

THE IDEALIST

While he wrote those poems
    of love, that won him fame,
she managed to deceive him
        with his best friend.

Later he took to drink,
    said cynicism is best,
yet every girl he had
        resembled the first.

BILLET DOUX

I'm thankful, Madam, that with lips and eyes
You did not play at other lovers' lies —

Those lies of 'love'... 'eternal'... 'only one'...
Hiding the bare bones of the skeleton.

But rather taking for granted bones are there
Covered them with your own flesh and hair.

So we forgot the loss age can't survive
in an intense hour of being still alive.

Unlike the young, who need excuse of fate,
You asked for no delay, the hour being late,

And with the pure deliberation of your will
Showed that the animal is human still.

We left each other feigning no pained regret
At having no life-sworn passion to forget.

PURE SPIRIT

Your lemony smell
on my pillow...

O little sea

You have left
perfume puddles
in the hollows of my bed

I will dream of divine thighs
and death by drowning.

THE WRITING

We talk to each other without significance,
        saying nothing.
I want to hear your conversation when you are alone.

I want to talk with myself yet have you hear me
        as if you were near me,
so that when you read me you can overhear me.

AIR ON THE G STRING
(FROM GOETHE)

Over all the hills,
not a sound,
among the trees you can hear
not a whisper around.
The birds are asleep in the trees.
Soon, soon, like these
you will sleep under ground.

NON GRIDATE PIU
(FROM GIUSSEPPE UNGARETTI)

Stop killing off the dead.
Stop your shouting, stop your noise
If you still want to hear them,
If you would live, not perish.

They speak in almost inaudible whispers,
They make no more sound
Than the growing grass,
Happy where no man walks.

FROM CATULLUS

Let us live, my Lesbia, let us love!
And all the mutterings of crabbed old men
weigh as dust, against this one reflection:
Suns can set, and they can return,
but we, once our short light has ended,
one long perpetual night must sleep.

TO A YOUNG WOMAN

You ask me whether you are beautiful
        in discontent.
There's many a woman asked this before you,
        my innocent!
And got no better answer than you do
        for compliment.

For know, there's one thing that a beauty
        must not know
for if she knew, who knows but she might put it
        on for show—
and even what is beautifullest, pride
        can overthrow.

I'd rather answer with a wondering look
        or with a stare.
And yet, for comfort, you may know that soon,
        too soon to care,
you'll know the answer, and can tell a friend
        that 'once' you were.

PROSPECT

The air is windy and pure
coming over the bluff of the mountain.

See, now, the sky with simplicity—

not to use, but to attain that vision
out of which, eventually, art may come.

CANTATA

The middle-aged
    can share disillusion
as the young share hope.

There is satisfaction in community.

The strange thing is that nobody makes good;
what they're after
       is the thing that fails.

All this effort
is part of the great experiment
something makes of us—
    the predicament we are in, accept.

ETERNAL BECOMING

We will what wants to become.

The noumenal beauty of women,
the ecstasies of birds,
the mind's inexplicable fertility—

all come into being out of the will to become.

A CIGARETTE IN SPACE-TIME

Of a transcendent beauty—
                    "Player's, Please"
shot in the night of time, from a train window.

Does it matter   what the forms convey?
And would pure *objets d'art*
                         have more to say?

What better than "Player's, Please?"
                    (waved in the cosmic wind)
to show our human universe
                    lost in eternity?

FOR RON EVERSON
(AFTER EZRA POUND, AND CONFUCIUS)

To love one's friends who make poems,
        is not that happiness?
To have them come from far places
back to the same old restaurant
        to read their six-line epics—
what could be more delightful?

FOR A.C.
(IN HER EVERYDAY CLOTHES)

Ah, darling, but you are fastidious!
        — an artist, crafting in the actual.
Let fools flutter their new plumage,
your mere presence transcends the fashion's fair:
an arrangement in grey, or brown,
        around a meditative mask,
your face, forever remote from mortality,
        you make an image of cloth and twine
eternal as the Nile, and lovely as a needle.

NEW YEAR

Every day begins a New Year,
as every place we are is here.

We are not scattered hour by hour
but always stay where we are:

even though myriad atoms fly
in and about, they pass us by.

We are quite still, we do not move—
watching them whirl, at one remove.

A RETURN

Sleep is our natural state of being—
                              an escape
from the tomfoolery of home-made illusions,
from the world of the senses, the invented code
          of light and shadow, dot and dash,
the running excited race, the procreative arena.

PROUST

It may be God takes such honey out of time
as bees from flowers—

the remembered sweet-cake and a view
of church spires.

THE MIND'S HEAVEN

The mind has its kingdom. It has its kingdom.
In the blue waters of a skyey imagination,
lingering at the buds of branches, and then gone
like a high bird, the mind
has its whitest circle, rarest kingdom;
has heaven, has the heaven of art,
has the heaven of true imagined love;
and in the blue waters, an unwritten future
of perfect lovers, of athletes,
and people.

A GAME OF CHANCE

Chance is the hand of God
Chance is where anything can happen.

To imitate nature you've got to write random poems
where "everything is possible" and
                    "nothing else is possible"

Like God, who likes to pretend ignorance.

IN SEPTEMBER

The heaving green like a crashing wave
                        has broken.
Rubble of black branches
and wave-worn hillsides appear.
The leaping crickets, the sleeping birds,
        grow silent.

Distant thunder threatens
A storm at sea.

One solitary fleck, a butterfly
hops from dry leaf to dry leaf
    looking for a flower.

from

NOTEBOOKS
1940-1994
(1994)

JACQUES CARTIER BRIDGE

An amusement park in the rain and fog,
      what courage there must be
to keep those entertainments alive
      in a world such as this:

the children trotting up to the "scenic railway"
      like a streak of blood,
while rolls of barbed wire cover the lot
      where the railway rides—

shrieking with joy through the fields of heaven
      but where in the end,
          as in all this world,
nothing is human but the music of despair.

COOL CATS

Cats listlessly
raising a paw against each other

know the boredom of things, if not the sadness,
      if not joy—

but men squabbling or
      in violent contest
forget the cool sweep
of eternity, in which all things
      unchangingly change.

GOLDEN AGE

To be young and famous is to hold a coloured bird by
        the tail feathers.

You're bound to lose it.
Everyone's a failure for the most of life,
        even the great ones.
Even the young and famous.

Success is for the golden age,
           if you get there.
And the world remembers only the success—
not the broken teeth, or the blood spattered on the stones.

from

THE CAGED TIGER
(1997)

BUTTERFLY

There is only one eternal love.
          And you must find her,
that one who makes it real for you,
once and for all, and then cleave to her
forever, for you will never find another.

          Butterfly,
whom, if you abandon, you will never find rest,
          or peace, never know Atlantis,
until you return to her, if a return is possible—
Or forever cry "Butterfly" from the far distance.*

LESSON

The poet says:
I exist only when you read me,
not when you praise.

You must read every line
                    for the tremor
in every word, in every phrase.

I have been sent
          to bring you light,
the poet says.

---

*   "O chiamerai Butterfly dalla lontana."

IT IS AN ART

It is an art   observing
       "the truth of human experience"

Directly or indirectly—does it matter?

So today, the individual
        is at the heart of it
As in the past, some god
      some universal truth
         was the aim.

Today the individual is at the heart of it.
You yourself.

You are the subject of poetry.

THIS ACTUAL

There is no idea as pleasant as this face.
No home in heaven as sure
        as this world of snow.

If it is incomplete, imperfect,
       that is a signature
of a higher possibility.

Accept the given
      as an oracle of a great mystery—
the obscure, the unknown,
     for its hidden message.

FOR A.J.M. SMITH

Like any animal coming into the world
unknowing, ignorant of what is now to come
                    or how it happens
man has believed always that something is hidden,
        that the real is not seen.

The transcendental then is merely the unknown;
but this does not change its meaning,
for if it were known it might add to our reality
                as much as those things
dreamed of by mystics, saints, and visionaries.

We gnaw at the mystery, extending knowledge.

I AM A LOST GLOVE

Darling,

this too-striking image is obviously
trying to steal the show,

I know, and it's a flaw, a defect,
        a thumb,

but nevertheless
    (though I say it poorly)—

I feel like a lost glove
            without you.

(Thank you for finding it.)

EARLY MORNING

Something that never was,
that now is
and that again will not be—

of which I am the observer
    (who will also not be)
but who observes as from an eternity
                of no time
the moment now,

the salesman who made a deal,
    the young woman who paid him,
the red-lipped college girls, bold, a bit shy,
        the counter girls on a coffee break,
                the macho men,

all milling about unconscious
         of one another
unconscious of the hand of time

that makes all things vanish, all fade,
    all suffer change.
And they live today as if they were forever,
    when they are here only for a day.

TRANSLATION
FROM ANACREON
TO DIONYSUS

Lord, with whom all-conquering Eros
     and the dark-eyed nymphs
  and also beauteous Aphrodite
play, you who wander about
     on the peaks of high mountains—
yea, I fall at your knees; come now with kindness
     toward us, and gratefully
       hear out our prayer:

Be a good counsellor to
    Kleobolus. And receive kindly,
this my love, O Deúnusos.

CHESS

There is a certain nobility
        in the way a computer loses.
Two games in two successive days,
             at level 4
(In the first he simply gave up his Queen,
     in the second moved a pawn, to be mated).
Mere arrangement of particles, by necessity,
               at the end.
        But it is noble.

So death is noble, a necessary rearrangement.
You "bow and accept the end"
          like a King.
The thing is, rearrangements are a foregone conclusion,
       a prepared event.
Necessity is the noble god—in which chance
            plays some part.
       Necessity says Yes.

We are the playthings of time, knowing too little
        and too much.
Clearly, we are a maker who plays the game
             but we are not
the Maker. We are in time's game, the rest—
we do not know, it is all arrangement
           and rearrangement.
      So far as we know.

But this game was predicted
          of necessity,
from the beginning, or some such game.
This game is as good as any, and will be played out
        to the end.
For all games on this board are chess,
         and chess is life
       that ends in Checkmate.

AS I SEE IT

"in una parte più e meno altrove..."

More in one place than in another
                    but not much anywhere, really
or almost none of it

A flicker, a flame, a transient trace
                                of epiphany,

not enough to cook an egg with
or to fertilize a fish

                    God is not mocked
Don't fool yourself
            There is no such thing
as another world, all found
or another being, all perfect
                    in some cold heaven
from which he could reach you

But there is something realized at every moment
            and vanishing in the void of time
that has its glory (another moment)
            in the music of Mozart or any kind act
            like feeding a stray cat

God is not a being, he is not it—or He, or She—
but a possibility, in the midst of chaos,
appearing with lightning presence
        even as blind chance *('Tuché)*,
                            a discovery
in all that darkness, now and again—
                    even as now
here in your face.

AN ENVOI

Go my song
Stand alone in the world
      (Do not expect praise)

Speak of the one true glory
    which is in art
    and human freedom

Realizing an unknown power
      but visible everywhere
invisible

Speak of the changing world
    as if timeless
    and everlasting

Do not seek praise
      nor flatter nor cajole

Avoid the young and the intolerant
    who are torn with envy
    and ambition

Stand in the first light of morning
    as sole witness
    to a difficult truth
    in an evil time.

from CONTINUATION III (Fragment)

Bless the quiet hour in the morning
           before the phone starts ringing
As you begin to recover you enjoy   the small pleasures
           cool water on your face
             bagels for breakfast
Like Mann, "living the life of luxury
           but nonetheless in pain"
The clichés of a lifetime   gathered together
        ...the spirit of the age
The mind of the many
         on which the sages writ
their thought arrested there, as a record
           until the next sage comes along.

io! io!
Light-hearing god
     of dawn
splendid daylight.
     To another life
another destiny I go.
Farewell,
    light that I love.
       io! io!

Iphigineia at Aulis.

There are days when

whatever *is is bright*

Sunt lumina

PHAINOMENA

that shine

All things that shine

that are glad

"for this we are made"

The glory simply in being

Bright

An Appearance   Erscheinung

not "mere appearance" but a shining

EPIPHANEIA

Phaos, light

out of *phaino*, to shine.

The lilacs falling over themselves
                on the garage roof,
and the trellis of trees, making their leaves
                for a new summer.
They ask no existentialist questions, do not consult Freud
        —whatever it is they do, they do.

Those mortal moments!
How to resurrect them for an eternity...
It is the seal of spirit
set upon matter
Khefre's scarab on the brow.

The imagined process   Tao
                        of the everliving soul

We seek in pattern
                the thing-in-itself

To be—
more than to live!

We have even learned to breathe
                            air.

Nothing is too strange to imagine
        A university on wheels, mobile books
        Poems that sing from your breakfast box

Who knows, the world may even improve...

Who the fuck cares what the ROC may want
        or be interested in[*]
This is not "The Poetry Game"
This is where we started
        and where we end,
saying one thing.

You can write yourself into a corner
        and then you're done,

---

[*]   In answer to the remark "Quebec writers do not know what the rest of Canada
       wants." Montreal poetry was typically outspoken. L.D.

But in eternity, they lose their perfume

    like cloves or garlic

or the sweetest flowers in Egyptian tombs.

So say to your art, live now,
                you too must die—
become the whitened bones or alabaster
        of a former life.

                Poem
live in the present, for you too must die.

The quotability of truth...
                   rely on that.

People know who is the liar
    Rely on that

See, the ducks running for cover
              to hide their heads in shame
There will be silence in those mountains...
Be still, my soul, be still

Amid the tomfoolery of ordinary illusions
            set sail
                   for the Far Point

by the golden star Arcturus,
        the only one visible
                in the grey-cast sky.

THE REAL AND
THE EPHEMERAL*
(FOR A.C.)

The way you sit, the way you speak, or walk
through the appearances of the world—
                              is an ephemeral art.

We see and love.

But to find lasting form,
to know the permanent in all change,
in the flicker of a smile, or in a frown,
        is the still greater glory.

---

*   Recent poem, here first published. L.D.